PUBLISHER'S NOTE

Ancient Chinese classic poems are exquisite works of art. As far as 2,000 years ago, Chinese poets composed the beautiful work *Book of Poetry* and *Elegies of the South*. Later, they created more splendid Tang poetry and Song lyrics. Such classic works as *Thus Spoke the Master* and *Laws Divine and Human* were extremely significant in building and shaping the culture of the Chinese nation. These works are both a cultural bond linking the thoughts and affections of Chinese people and an important bridge for Chinese culture and the world.

Mr. Xu Yuanchong has been engaged in translation for 70 years. He won the Lifetime Achievement Award in Translation conferred by the Translators Association of China (TAC) in 2010, and won the "Aurora Borealis" Prize for Outstanding Translation of Fiction Literature, conferred by the Federation of International Translators (FIT) in 2014. He is honored as the only expert who translates Chinese poems into both English and French. After his excellent interpretation, many Chinese classic poems have been further refined into perfect English and French rhymes. This collection of Classical Chinese Poetry and Prose gathers his most representative English translations. It includes the classic works *Thus Spoke the Master*, *Laws Divine and Human* and dramas such as *Romance of the Western Bower*, *Dream in Peony Pavilion*, *Love in Long-life Hall* and *Peach Blooms Painted with Blood*. The largest part of the collection includes the translation of selected poems from different dynasties. The selection includes various types of poetry. The selected works start from the pre-Qin era to the Qing Dynasty, covering almost the entire history of classic poems in China. Reading these works is like tasting "living water from the source" of Chinese culture.

We hope this collection will help English readers "understand, enjoy and delight in" Chinese classic poems, share the intelligence of Confucius and Lao Tzu (the Older Master), share the gracefulness of Tang poems, Song lyrics and classic operas and songs and promote exchanges between Eastern and Western culture. We also sincerely invite precious suggestions from our readers.

出版前言

　　中国古代经典诗文是中国传统文化的奇葩。早在两千多年以前，中国诗人就写出了美丽的《诗经》和《楚辞》；以后，他们又创造了更加灿烂的唐诗和宋词。《论语》《老子》这样的经典著作，则在塑造、构成中华民族文化精神方面具有极其重要的意义。这些作品既是联接所有中国人思想、情感的文化纽带，也是中国文化走向世界的重要桥梁。

　　许渊冲先生从事翻译工作70年，2010年荣获"中国翻译文化终身成就奖"，2014年荣获国际译联颁发的"北极光"杰出文学翻译奖。他被称为将中国诗词译成英法韵文的唯一专家，经他的妙手，许多中国经典诗文被译成出色的英文和法文韵语。这套"许译中国经典诗文集"荟萃许先生最具代表性的英文译作，既包括《论语》《老子》这样的经典著作，又包括《西厢记》《牡丹亭》《长生殿》《桃花扇》等戏曲剧本，数量最多的则是历代诗歌选集。这些诗歌选集包括诗、词、散曲等多种体裁，所选作品上起先秦，下至清代，几乎涵盖了中国古典诗歌的整个历史。阅读和了解这些作品，即可尽览中国文化的"源头活水"。

　　我们希望这套许氏译本能使英语读者对中国经典诗文也"知之，好之，乐之"，能够分享孔子、老子的智慧，分享唐诗、宋词、中国古典戏曲的优美，并以此促进东西文化的交流。也敬请读者朋友提出宝贵意见。

PROJECT FOR TRANSLATION AND PUBLICATION
OF CHINESE CULTURAL WORKS
中国文化著作翻译出版工程项目

CLASSICAL CHINESE POETRY AND PROSE

GOLDEN TREASURY OF
SONG, YUAN, MING AND QING POETRY

TRANSLATED BY XU YUANCHONG
& FRANK M. XU

许译中国经典诗文集

宋元明清诗选 | 许渊冲　许明　译

五洲传播出版社
China Intercontinental Press

中华书局
Zhonghua Book Company

CONTENTS
目　　录

11

13

17

Ming Dynasty

明 代

21

CLASSICAL CHINESE POETRY AND PROSE

GOLDEN TREASURY OF
SONG, YUAN, MING AND QING POETRY

TRANSLATED BY XU YUANCHONG
& FRANK M. XU

China Intercontinental Press   Zhonghua Book Company

Preface

Music moulds character, and therefore shares in determining social and political issues. When the modes of music change, the fundamental laws of the state change with them. —Plato
Let me write the songs of a nation, and I care not who makes its laws.
—Daniel O'Connell
"We can understand a people, best through their poetry," said Robert Payne in his *White Pony,* "and the Chinese who have written poetry since the beginning of time have always regarded poetry as the finest flower of their culture.... They have written more poetry than all the other nations of the earth put together."

I

The Tang Dynasty (618–906) and the Song Dynasty (960–1279) were the Golden Age and the Silver Age of Chinese literature, not only of Chinese but also of world literature, for during the Dark Ages in the West, the Tang and the Song Empire attained the highest political, economic and cultural development not only in the East but also in the whole world. If the reader is interested in the greatest empires that had ruled over the greatest country in the world for more than six centuries, it would not be uninteresting to read Tang and Song poetry, which might reveal the secret of the highest and the longest-established civilization in world history. This secret may be summed up in two words, that is, rite and music. Music imitates the harmony of nature and rite imitates the order of the universe. Rite is instituted to secure the mean in man's desire and music (including poetry) the mean in man's sentiment. Rite and music in Confucius' system are even more important than gymnastics and music in Plato's system, for rite is to regulate man's mind, music to harmonize man's affection, government to promote their performance and law to guard against their violation. In comparison with rite and music, government and law are but secondary, for their main function is but to provide the conditions that make rite and music possible. That may be said to be the gist of Confucian philosophy of government, of which the reader can catch some glimpses in this Golden Treasury of Tang and Song poetry.

If the Tang poets imitated the order of the universe as they imitated the harmony of nature, that is to say, they were emotional in imitating both, then the Song poets may be said to imitated the former more than the latter, that is to say, they were more rational and less emotional than their predecessors. After the song of the Tang poets came the logic of the Song philosopher: the first emphasized appreciation and the second understanding. The best-known poets of the Northern Song Dynasty were Su Shi (1037–1101) and Huang Tingjian (1045–1105). We may read, for instance, one of Su's poems on Mount Lu:

> It's a range viewed in face and peaks viewed from the side,
> Assuming different shapes viewed from far and wide.
> Of Mountain Lu we cannot make out the true face,
> For we are lost in the heart of the very place.

If the first couplet leads us to appreciate the beauty of nature, then the second leads us to understand the order of the universe. Strange to say, the understanding of the order of the human world might lead to disaster. For example, we may read another of Su's poems written after the death of the old emperor and on the ascension to the throne of the new in 1085:

> The crop still bears a plentiful harvest this year;
> I feel myself already free from worldly care.
> On my way back from the Temple good news I hear;
> Even wild flowers and song birds have a cheerful air.

In this quatrain we may find harmony between nature and man, and by "good news" the poet meant the new emperor's ascension; put his political enemy in power interpreted the "good news" as the death of the old emperor and the poet was exiled far, far away from the capital. This may serve to show how much more the Song Dynasty emphasized the order of the human world than the harmony of nature.

This may further be illustrated by poems of the same theme written by Tang and Song poets. Let us compare A Farewell Song by Wang Wei and another by Huang Tingjian written on a picture of farewell drawn by Li Longmian:

> (Tang) No dust is raised on pathways wet with morning rain;
> The willows by the tavern look so fresh and green.
> I would ask you to drink a cup of wine again;
> West of the Sunny Pass no more friends will be seen.
> (Song) After heart-broken songs the wayfarer's unseen;
> The silent picture presents a heart-breaking scene.
> What will he see on his way west of Sunny Pass?
> Only the cattle when north wind blows down the grass.
> Of all the human griefs the parting one lasts long;
> Longmian makes a picture of heart-breaking song.

The tavern willows have nothing to gnaw their heart;

'Tis the grief of those who are unwilling to part.

In the Tang poem the tavern willows seem to be unwilling be part with the wayfarer and try to retain him by their beauty freshness and greenness. This is a tradition inherited from *the Book of Poetry* (See *A Homesick Warrior*). This also shows there is harmony between man and nature and the poet tries to make the tree empathetic and sympathetic with man. In the Song poem the tavern willows have nothing to gnaw their heart; this shows the poet more objective than subjective, he appeals to the understanding more than to the imagination, he emphasizes truth more than beauty. On the other hand, in the Tang poem west of the Sunny Pass no more friends will be seen, this is the subjective reason why the poet asks his friend to drink on more cup of wine, while in the Song poem west of the Sunny Pass the wayfarer may find the cattle when the north wind blows down the grass, that is only an objective description of the natural scenery without any personal feeling involved in it. That is one of the main differences between Tang and Song poetry.

As the Song empire was not so strong and powerful as the Tang, it had to emphasize the order of the human world rather than the harmony between man and nature. When the capital of the Northern Song Dynasty was occupied by Jurchen invaders, the well-known poetess Li Qingzhao wrote the following poem:

Be man of men while you're alive;

Be soul of souls e'en if you're dead.

Think of Xiang Yu who'd not survive

His men whose blood for him was shed!

The first two lines appeal to our understanding and reason and the last two to our imagination and emotion. Xiang Yu (232–202 B.C.) was a general who led his soldiers to fight for the throne, won a hundred battles but lost the last decisive one and killed himself for he was ashamed to survive the soldiers who had given their lives for him. Glorification of the defeated hero instead of the victor shows also the love of peace and order of the Chinese People. The Song empire was overthrown by the Tartar invaders, but the Tartars were at last assimilated to Chinese culture.

There was a legend that Confucius went to ask the Old Master for advice on the rite. The Old Master said nothing but opened his mouth. Come back, Confucius thought it over and understood at last that by showing the tongue in his toothless mouth, the Old Master meant the soft would last longer than the hard just as the tongue outlasted the tooth. Then he came to the conclusion that a State should not be armed to the teeth and ruled by strength and power but by rite and music. Whence the Confucius' motto: Do not do to others what you would not have others do to you. On the other hand, we may find in the *Bible,* motto of Jesus: Do to others what you would have others do to you. It seems that Confucius was negative and passive while Jesus was positive and active. Here lies the fundamental difference between Oriental and Occidental civilization. In accordance with Jesus' teaching, if you are a Christian, you should christianize the pagan, then you are doing what you would have others do to you. In accordance with Confucius' teaching, if you go to a pagan country, you should follow the pagan custom, then you are not imposing your own will upon others. Adopting Confucius' motto, China has been ruled for thousands of years by rite and music without waging aggressive war on other countries. This political policy is reflected in the following verse by Du Fu:

> Slaughter shan't go beyond its sphere;
>
> Each State should have its own frontier.
>
> If an invasion is repelled.
>
> Why shed more blood unless compelled?

If the Occidental countries should assimilate some Oriental philosophy and poetry to their civilization just as the Oriental countries have assimilated Occidental science and technology to theirs, there would be a peaceful and happier world in the coming centuries.

II

How to understand the Chinese people through the Yuan poetry? In 1271 the Song Dynasty was overthrown by the Mongols and the Yuan Dynasty was established in the Central Plain. Under the Mongol reign the intellectuals were reduced to the second lowest position in society, so their discontent was revealed in a nostalgia of the bygone days and criticism against the rulers of the overthrown empire. For example, we may read Zhao Mengfu's verse on General Yue Fei, who tried to recover the lost land and was sentenced to death by the Song emperor fleeing to the south.

> What is the use of regretting the hero's death ?
>
> How could half of the divided country last long?

For another example, we may cite Yu Ji's "on Premier Wen Tianxiang", who was captured by the Mongol army and executed in the capital (modern Beijing).

> In vain you wielded spear to raise the setting sun.
>
> How could a Southern captive stop the north wind's run!

Here we see the setting sun alludes to the overthrown Song empire and the north wind to the Mongol forces.

Since the intellectuals could not rise in arms against the Mongol rulers, they could only write poetry about life of hermits and beauty of nature. For instance, we may read Jie Xisi's verse on a moonlit night:

> I shiver not with cold dew nor cold breeze
> But watch the moon grow round o'er shady trees....
> East of my garden wall two poplars long
> Fill lonely room with lonely autumn song.

Here the poet shivered not with cold but with the oppression of the rulers, so he wished to see the moon grow round, for the waxing and waning moon symbolized a country's rise and fall. The round moon was his ideal but the reality was two lonely poplars whose rustling leaves seemed to fill his lonely room with lonely autumn songs.

On the other hand, there were Mongol poets who sang the praise of the peaceful life under the Mongol reign, and the most remarkable among them was Sa Dula, whose frontier songs read as follows:

> 1. At sunset here and there disperse cattle and sheep;
>   The cheese is all the sweeter mingled with grass's scent.
> 2. It's hard to bend the bow in high wind at Great Wall,
>   But the young lords on hunting ground ride left and right.
> 3. The Northern beauty is sixteen,
>   With rosy face and eyebrows green.
>   The road is fragrant with her steed;
>   Short whip in hand, she rides with speed.

The first couplet describes the peaceful life in the grassland, the second the hunting young lords and the third the Northern beauty who also rode with speed like young men. Besides, we have Yu Ji's verse on the grandeur of the imperial train:

> The golden sunlight makes imperial robe more red;
>
> In royal progress His Majesty rides ahead.
>
> At dawn the steep sky-scraping path retains the cars;
>
> At night the guards with bows stand round the tents like stars.

These verses have perhaps revealed the reason why the militant Mongol tribe could defeat and overthrow the weakened Southern Song empire.

So far as the style is concerned, the Yuan poets admired and imitated Tang poetry and criticized and improved on Song verse. For instance, we may see Guan Yunshi's admiration for Li Bai (701–762) in his "Peach Blossom Mountain", where the immortal poet was said to have dwelled and written poems on peach blossoms.

> Spring comes to life when fragrance spreads from mountains proud;
>
> His fingers crush the rainbow into powder fine.

Yang Weizhen's admiration for Li Bai went even further and higher in his "Waterfall of Mount Lu":

> Thirsty for wine at night, what could he do but try
>
> To ride the whale and drink the sea till it goes dry?
>
> The water drunk turns to endless cataract here,
>
> Hanging like jade rainbow over abyss cold and clear.

But on the other hand, admiration did not bind Yuan poets to slavish imitation in face of altered circumstances. For example, we may compare Guan Yunshi's fisherman with Liu Zongyuan's (773–819):

> Liu: A straw-cloaked man afloat, behold!
>
> Is fishing snow on river cold.

> Guan: Don't envy silken quilt on which the lovebirds sing!
>
> In a fisherman's song there is another spring.

Liu's fisherman was lofty because he was proud of his straw cloak while Guan's was happy because he thought his quilt of reed catkins better than a silken one. We may further compare Sa Dula's "The Lady of Stone" with Wang Jian's (768–833):

> Wang: waiting for him alone
>
> > Where the river goes by,
> >
> > She turns into a stone
> >
> > Gazing with longing eye.
>
> Sa: The gentle wind spreads snowflakes to powder her face;
>
> > The sun will rouge her cheeks by melting dewdrops bright.
> >
> > Don't say there is no mirror to reflect her grace!
> >
> > The moon will shine on the Lady of Stone all night.

On reading Wang's verse, the reader will be sympathetic with the Lady of Stone, while in Sa's verse even the sun, the moon and snowflakes become sympathetic.

If Yuan poets did well in imitating Tang poetry, then they might be said to have outdone the Song poets. For instance, if we compare Chen Fu's "To the Temple of Golden Hill" with Su Shi's (1037–1101):

> Su: Thanking the god, I say I'm reluctant to stay,
>
> > If I won't go home, like these waves I'll pass away.
>
> Chen: Bowing, you drink on boundless waves celestial light;
>
> > There is another heaven and earth on your height.

We may find the former more rational and the latter more emotional. This may be further illustrated by comparing Su's famous "West Lake" with Yang

Weizhen's poem:

> Su: The West Lake Looks like the Fair lady at her best,
>> Whether she is richly adorned or plainly dressed.
> Yang: Below the Bride of Stone the waves blend with the sky;
>> Beyond Mount Eagle tower many mountains high.
>> I'd wait for you until I die like the stone bride.
>> O when will you fly like Mount Eagle to my side?

The Yuan poem's emotion is stronger than the Song couplet's. From the above-cited examples, we may see the progress made by Yuan poets in their verse writing.

But Yuan poets made still greater progress in their dramatic songs than in their poetry. The best-known Yuan drama was Wang Shifu's *Romance of the Western Bower*, of which we may read the lovemaking and parting scenes.

> Act IV, Scene 1, the hero sings:
>
> Spring comes on earth with flowers dyed,
> Her willowy waist close by my side,
> Her pistil plucked, my dewdrop drips
> And her peony sips
> With open lips.
>
> Act IV, Scene 3, the heroine sings:
>
> It's my regret
> So late we met;
> It grieves my heart
> So soon to part.
> Long as the willow branch may be,
> It cannot tie his parting steed to the tree.

What would I not have done

If autumn forest could hang up the setting sun?

It is noteworthy that this tragedy was written two or three hundred years before Shakespeare wrote his *Romeo and Juliet*. Thus we may come to the conclusion that, east or west, poetic minds think alike.

III

In 1368 the Yuan Dynasty was overthrown by the uprising armies and the Ming Dynasty was founded. As the first Ming emperor was an uneducated monk, he did not think highly of the intellectuals and treated them unfairly. This was pointed out in this poem:

The emperor of lords made light and ministers.

For example, Liu Ji who helped the emperor to overthrow the Yuan Dynasty and won an earldom was put to death by a false charge, so he wrote in his verse:

Why should the silkworm, busy alone and forget

It will be boiled when its cocoon is made...?

As a result, many intellectuals preferred hermitage to service in the court. For instance, Gao Qi wrote the following verse to the mume blossoms:

A hermit lives in mountains covered by snow white;

A beauty comes to the grove when the moon shines bright.

The shivering bamboo lends you its shadow slender;

The outspread moss would hide your fragrant petals tender.

But little did he dream that the outspread moss could not hide his fragrance and he was put to death because his satirical poems had offended the emperor. Other intellectuals pretended to be mad so as to escape disaster.

For example, Zhu Yunming wrote the following verse:

> Not in proper attire and with disheveled hair,...
> I walk in corridor to and fro, here and there.
> At mid-court I lie down and look upwards carefree
> As fish swimming around fairy isles in the sea.

Tang Yin, son of a rich merchant of Suzhou, who won the first honor in district examinations at the age of sixteen and in provincial examinations at twenty-nine, wrote such clever lines as:

> Others may pity me so foolish and so mad;
> I laugh at them for those who can't see through are sad...
>
> I seek no drink divine nor meditation deep;
> Hungry, I take my meal and tired, I go to sleep.
> I live on selling verse and pictures as I please;
> I rove among red flowers and green willow trees...
> I drank till drunk as often as I enjoy pleasure;
> An immortal on earth, I love my life of leisure.

On the other hand, there were intellectuals who were not afraid of death. The most remarkable among them was Yu Qian, minister of war who had beaten the foe but was put to death after the emperor's restoration. He wrote in his "Song to the Lime":

> You come out of deep mountains after hammer blows;
> Under fire and water tortures you're not in woes.
> Though broken into pieces, you will have no fright;
> You'll purify the world by washing it ever white.

It was the poet himself who made light of hammer blows and of fire and water tortures he had suffered just as the lime did. How could he be fearless?

Read another quatrain of his:

> I tell those who roam
>
> To make light of cold.
>
> Spring wind will soon come
>
> Eastwards as foretold.

He was not afraid of the cold for he knew beforehand that spring wind would bring warmth to the world. Is it not interesting to compare the last couplet with that of Shelley's "Ode to the West Wind" written four hundred years later?

Politically, intellectuals had suffered persecution under the Ming reign. Economically, commerce and trade had developed and prosperity was enjoyed in such cities as Suzhou, capital of the ancient kingdom Wu, as shown in the following verse of Tang Yin's:

> The capital of Wu is earthly paradise;
>
> As Western Gate nowhere's so prosperous and nice.
>
> Three thousand green-sleeved beauties upstair and downstair;
>
> From dawn to dusk the market uproar runs ever high;...

Militarily, anti-Japanese generals and soldiers were glorified as seen in the following couplet taken from "General Qi's Sword":

> Can thousand coins of gold buy a sword of this kind ?
>
> Each inch of steel reveals a battle-hardened mind.

And General Qi's army was described in his own quatrain "March at Dawn":

> Our banners undulate along the winding stream
>
> Without disturbing the riverside birds from their dream.

Artistically, Ming poets continued to imitate Tang poetry and improve on Song verse. For instance, we may compare Yuan Kai's couplet with Du Fu's (712–770):

> Du: The boundless forest sheds its leaves shower by shower;
>
> Then endless river rolls its waves hour after hour.
>
> Yuan: Leaves fall shower by shower on the river long.
>
> The wild geese pierce the midnight rain with their new song.

Yuan's verse is not so regular as Du's, but the wild geese's song adds something new to the sad breath of autumn. For another example, we may read Du Fu's and Yang Ji's verse on the Yueyang Tower:

> Du: War's raging on the northern frontier;
>
> Leaning on rails, I shed sad tears.
>
> Yang: The queen's soul comes awake...
>
> Wind and rain weep for her sake.

Du's verse is realistic in describing his own sorrow, while Yang's is romantic by saying that even wind and rain would weep for the queen drowned in the Dongting Lake two thousand years ago.

As for the improvement made by Ming poets on Song verse, we may compare the following philosophic lines by Su Shi and by Wang Shouren:

> Su: Of Mountain Lu we cannot make out the true face
>
> For we are lost in the heart of the very place.
>
> Wang: The weal and woe which stay not in mind will pass by
>
> Just as the floating cloud sailing across the sky.

Su's verse is like the plain-dressed lady while Wang's like a richly-adorned beauty. If we compare this verse of Su's with Yang Jisheng's "On Mount Tai",

> The world's small east to west
>
> When I climb mountains high.
>
> I look up from the crest:
>
> Higher white clouds sail by.

We may say both are plainly-dressed beauties, but Su is narrative while Yang is suggestive: high as the mountains are, there is something still higher, that is, white cloud. Yang seems not so straight-forward as Su is. Here we see the improvement made by Ming poets on their predecessors.

But intellectuals of the Ming Dynasty made greater progress in novels and in dramatic songs than in poetry. One of the well-known novels was Wu Chengen's *Jourrney to the West*. Read his verse on "The Autumn Moon", and you can get a glimpse of his rich imagination.

> Moon, will you drink a cup of wine
>
> To her loneliness as to mine?

One of the well-known tragedies was Tang Xianzu's *Dream in Peony Pavilion*. Here we may read Feng Xiaoqing's verse on reading Tang's tragedy:

> How can I bear to hear cold rain beat window panes?
>
> I light my lamp to read *Pavilion of Peony*.
>
> The beauty died of love, in dreams she still remains;
>
> She's not so lonely, heart-broken as dreamless me.

Judging by Feng's quatrain, we can see the influence exercised by Tang Xianzu on his contemporaries and on posterity.

IV

In 1644 the peasant army occupied the Ming capital and captured and raped the favorite mistress of General Wu Sangui, commander-in-chief of the Seaside Mountain Pass of the Great Wall. Burning with wrath, General Wu led the Manchurian forces to recapture the capital and his mistress, resulting in the downfall of the Ming and the establishment of the Qing Dynasty. This was recorded in Wu Weiye's epic poem, "Song of the Beautiful Yuanyuan", which was meant to be a satire against General Wu.

> (1) The royal armies dressed in mourning shed their tears;
>   The wrathful general for his lady wielded his spears.
> (2) Had not our general beaten the rebel force,
>   How could his lady fair be rescued on a horse?
> (3) His family were slain and turned to dust and clay;
>   Her rosy face will shine in history for aye.

A general should fight for the country, but General Wu fought only for his beloved lady. Here lies the satire of this poem. The contrast between the general and his army, between his love for his mistress and his hatred against the rebel force, between his family's death and his lady's life was meant to make the satire keener. But in the west Antony's loss of an empire for the Egyptian queen was considered as "the world well lost" by Dryden, so the western reader may not perceive the satire of this verse. Anyhow, it marks the development made by Qing poets on the historical poem "Everlasting Regret" of the Tang Dynasty.

Another beauty as well-known as Yuanyuan was the poetess Liu Rushi. At first, she fell in love with the patriotic poet Chen Zilong, who admired her beauty as well as her poetry:

> The weeping willows stand east of the curtained bowers;
> Orioles and butterflies pass through the faded flowers.
> But peach blossoms on Cold Food Day are beautified
> By beauties living or buried by the lakeside.

The weeping willows and faded flowers in West Lake symbolize the overthrown Ming Dynasty and the beauties living or dead refer to heroes and heroines, including herself. Since the intellectuals who said or did anything against the rulers were put to death (i.e., Jin Shengtan), so poets dared not express their regret for the downfall of the Ming Dynasty but allude to it in terms of trees, flowers and bowers. For another example, we may read Wang Shizhen's quatrain "On River Qinhuai":

> For years my broken, heart yearns for a sail in vain;
> My dreams still haunt the riverside bower of yore.
> The days are veiled in sheet of wind and threads of rain;
> Spring's gloomy scene looks like late autumn to deplore.

Here the wind and rain hint at the Manchurian rule and the sail at the poet's hope.

But for Manchurian poets, the downfall of the Ming was not to be regretted nor deplored, for it was neither the generals nor the intellectuals but the Ming emperors indulged in pleasures were to blame. For instance, Nalan Xingde wrote the following couplet in his "On the Capital of Yore":

> The Northern kings sought pleasure on the Southern shore;
> The bygone dynasties need no grass to deplore.

So, by and by poets turned their sympathy from the overthrown Dynasty to the oppressed people. The most remarkable poet was Zheng Xie, who wrote the following well-known couplet :

> I listen in my office to rustling bamboo;
> It seems to complain of its woe as people do.

No less remarkable was the versatile poet Yuan Mei. He said openly that the separation between man and wife in Stone Moat Village deserved more sympathy than that between king and queen in the Palace.

> In Stone Moat Village when the man parted from his wife,
> More tears were shed than in the palace of Long Life.

Sometimes, he wrote with humorous satire:

> The chickens eat their fill;
> They're boiled when fat they grow.
> The feeder's wise and will
> Not let the chickens know.

This shows that he was wiser than the ruler and would not grow fat lest he should be boiled. Worldly wisdom was combined with simple and delightful language, which shows his improvement on rational verse of his Song predecessors. His quatrain on verse writing shows his art of creation. His verse "On Pushing Open the Window" shows his love of nature just as "The Chickens" shows his love of freedom, and his elegy on his wise mistress shows his love of beauty and wisdom. In short, through his poetry we can understand a typical Chinese intellectual.

But intellectuals of the Qing Dynasty made not so much progress in poetry as in novel and in drama. The best novel in Chinese history was Cao Xueqin's *Dream of Red Mansions*, from which "Lin Daiyu's Elegy on Flowers" is selected:

> Oh, in the three hundred and sixty days each year
> The cutting wind and biting frost make flowers sear!
> How long can their fragrant blossoms last fresh and fair?
> Once when they're blown away, they can be found nowhere.

In this elegy we find Cao's love for flowers or beauty is even deeper than Yuan Mei's.

The best-known drama of the Qing Dynasty was Hong Sheng's *Love in Long-life Hall*, of which the prologue begins as follows:

> Since olden days how few
> Lovers have remained ever true!

If they love each other heart and soul,

They'd be united from pole to pole.

A thousand miles could not keep them apart;

Not even death could sever heart from heart.

In this prologue we find love much more highly glorified than in Yuan Mei's Elegy.

Another drama almost as well-known as Hong's *Long-life Hall* was Kong Shangren's *Peach Blossoms painted with Blood*. After reading it, Chen Yuwang blamed the last ruler of the Ming Dynasty because

He loves a beautiful woman more than his land.

This might be said to be the cause of the empire's downfall. Besides novel and drama, the Qing Dynasty could still boast of the best short stories of ghost written by Pu Songling.

The opium war in 1840 marked the beginning of China's modern age. Lin Zexu, national hero who burned the opium imported from England, was banished to the northwest frontier. Though in exile, he still showed his love of the country in the following verse:

The hundred-foot-high Great Wall bars the western sky;

The endless battlements join proud trees far and nigh.

His patriotic spirit exercised great influence on posterity. Gong Zizhen, the most important Qing poet since 1840, proffered service to Lin Zexu and left the court when he was rejected. Though out of court, he still. wrote such patriotic verses as:

(1) The fallen blossoms are not an unfeeling thing;

Though turned to mud, they'd nurture flowers' growth next spring.

(2) From wind and thunder comes a nation's vital force,

What a great pity not to hear a neighing horse!

The last Qing emperor of the 19th century tried to adopt reformative policies, but he was forced by the imperial dowager to put to death the reformists, among whom Tan Sitong, who wrote the following prophetic verse in 1891 when he climbed the highest peak in Hunan:

> Beyond dark earth stars sink awake;
>
> The sun leaps up like molten gold.
>
> From half the spoon of Dongting Lake
>
> Dragon would rise in autumn cold.

The dark earth refers to the Qing empire and the sun and dragon seem to predict the rise of Mao Zedong born in 1893 near the Dongting Lake. Strange to say, Mao wrote the first lines of his first poem in 1925 as follows:

> Alone I stand in autumn cold
>
> Where River Xiang goes north, behold!

Poets who died after 1911 are not included in this anthology, but through the poetry selected and translated here, we can understand the life, love and dreams of the Chinese people.

Xu Yuanchong

Peking University

January 2009

SONG DYNASTY
(960–1279)

Chen Tuan (?—989)

MY HERMITAGE[①]

I've left trace in the vanity fair for ten years;

Turning my head, I find blue hill in dream appears.

A sound sleep will do me more good than vanity;

The rich in red mansions would fall in poverty.

I'm grieved to know that swords can't save the king at stake,

Nor can the flute and songs keep the drunkard awake.

To my old hermitage old book and lute I'll bring;

Wild flowers and singing birds herald the same spring.

---

① This is a pastoral poem in praise of man's communion with nature.

Liu Kai (947—1000)

ON THE FRONTIER

A hissing arrow flies straight a thousand feet high;

It makes a drier sound in windless tranquil sky.

Three hundred greenish-pupiled Tartar cavaliers

All gaze upon the cloud, bridling their golden gears.

Wang Yucheng (954–1001)

IN BANISHMENT

My horse threads its way through the aster-yellowed mountains;
I give free rein to horse and fancy on the run.
In thousands of ravines the evening sings with fountains;
So many peaks stand silent in the setting sun.
Leaves fallen, crab apples reveal their rosy hue;
Field buckwheat in flower looks like fragrant white snow.
How, after crooning, could I feel sorrow anew?
House, bridge, plain, trees remind me of the land I know.

THE MOURNING DAY①

With nor flowers nor wine I passed the Mourning Day,
As drear as a friar begging all the way.
I asked my neighbor tor new-made fire last night,
Lighting my lamp at dawn, I may read by its light.

---

① The Cold Food Day fell three days before the Mourning Day when
people were forbidden to make fire, so a poor scholar should ask his
neighbor for new-made fire or he could not light his lamp for reading.
This quatrain shows the diligence of ancient Chinese scholars.

Yang Pu

THE DOUBLE SEVENTH EVE[1]

I do not know what has the Cowherd in his heart.

Why should he ask his Maid to weave a work of art?

From year to year the artful world asks to be clever;

The clever will do good, but the artful will never.

---

[1] The Cowherd and the Weaving Maid were believed to be two stars in love who were allowed to meet once every year on the seventh day of the seventh lunar month. It was a folk custom for women to pray to the Weaving Star that they be clever if they succeed in threading a needle. This quatrain is a satire on the artful but not clever world.

Kou Zhun (962—1023)

ON THE RIVER

On endless waves along the broad shore sparse masts tower;

Leaning alone against the rails, my thoughts wild run.

Beyond the trees with leaves falling shower by shower,

The autumn hills are half crowned with the setting sun.

Lin Bu (968–1028)

TO THE MUME BLOSSOM

You bloom alone when flowers fade out far and near;

You queen it over all the garden day and night.

Sparse shadows slant across the shallow water clear

And gloomy fragrance floats at dusk in dim moonlight.

Seeing your purity, white birds alight and peer;

Knowing your sweetness, butterflies would lose their heart.

Only a lucky poet's your companion dear.

Put sandal clappers and golden goblets apart!①

---

① Singers with sandal clappers and drinkers with golden goblets are not good companions.

Fan Zhongyan (989–1052)

THE FISHERMAN ON THE STREAM

You go up and down stream;

You love to eat the bream.

Lo! the fishing boat braves

Perilous wind and waves.

Yan Shu (991—1055)

TO ONE UNNAMED

Your fragrant cab has never again come in sight.

Like traceless clouds in royal dreams wafting where they please.

The courtyard white with pear blossoms steeped in moonlight,

The pond is rippled by willow down in the breeze.

So many lonely hours cannot be drowned in wine;

I feel all the more desolate on Cold Food Day.[1]

How can I send you letters or even a line?

Everywhere mountains and rivers bar the way.

---

[1] According to Chinese custom, fire was forbidden and cold food was eaten two days before the Day of Mourning for the Dead, that is, the eighth day of the third lunar month.

Song Qi (998–1061)

TO THE FALLEN FLOWER

Your blossoms red and petals white fall with regret

To part from mist-veiled mansions green you can't forget.

Before you reach the ground, you dance in wind with grace;

Fallen, you still reveal your half-hidden fair face.

The sea sheds pearly tears when sailors go ashore;

The beauty's remains smell sweet though she is no more.

You cannot leave your honey to the butterflies.

Confide your sweet heart to beehives before it dies!

Mei Yaochen (1002–1060)

ROVING IN THE MOUNTAINS

It suits my roving mood

To see hills high and low.

Peaks change their shapes, all good;

Astray in Woods I go.

Up a tree climbs a bear;

At a creek drinks a doe.

But where's the village? Where?

Clouds vibrate with cock's crow.

Ouyang Xiu (1007–1072)

REPLY TO A BANISHED FRIEND[1]

I am afraid the vernal wind here will not blow;

In second moon no hillside flowers have come out.

But oranges grow on trees bowed with lingering snow,

And bamboo shoots startled by frozen thunder sprout.

I am homesick to hear homing wild geese at night;

Though in poor health, I feel the reviving new year.

We had our days in capital of flowers bright.

Why should we lament when wild blossoms come late here?

---

[1] This poem describes the poet's friendship for a banished official.

BEFORE THE PAVILION

The mountains green are dappled with red leaves, behold!

At sunset out of sight the verdant meadows spread.

Visitors do not care that spring will soon grow old;

On fallen blooms before the pavilion they tread.

WRITTEN IN DREAM

A flute has chilled the moon over a thousand hills;
Dim sight is dazzled by a hundred daffodils.
After a game of chess, the world has changed its face;
Sobered from wine, can one not miss his native place?

Su Shunqin (1008–1049)

PASSING BY SUZHOU

The Coiling Dragon Gate affords a striking sight:
After a drizzling rain the weather's fine again.
The willows green enjoy their ease with egrets white;
The distant hills and streams might share our joy and pain.
It's up to Heaven to rule o'er our rise and fall;
We should make light of sufferings from day to day.
I am not born to enjoy lovely scenes at all;
Even at dusk my lonely boat should sail away.

Li Gou (1009–1059)

NOSTALGIA

The sun is said to set at the end of the earth;

I see the setting sun but I can't find my hearth.

My homeward way is barred by green, green mountains proud;

The mountains are again veiled by the evening cloud.

Shao Yong(1011–1077)

SONG OF FLOWER SPRAY①

The flower spray on my head reflected in the wine,

From my wine cup upsurges a spray of flower fine.

I've lived in time of peace as long as sixty years,

And seen four reigns of prosperity with my peers.

Moreover, I am still in good health, safe and sound.

How can I miss the flowers in full bloom all around?

The flower's shadow reddens my wine where it's sunk.

How can I leave these blossoms without getting drunk?

---

① The poet is a philosopher. This poem describes the time of peace and
   prosperity in which people should make merry while they can.

Wen Tong (1018–1079)

THE MOON VIEWED AFTER RAIN IN THE MOUNTAIN

The sparse pines sieve moonbeams
And weave shadows like dreams.
Loitering thereamong,
I cannot sleep for long.
Lotus leaves roll in breeze;
Rain o'er, fruits fall from trees.
Who'd sing with me or brood?
Crickets' songs fill the wood.

Zeng Gong (1019–1083)

THE WEST TOWER

The billows come and go like cloud;
The north wind blows up thunder loud.
All curtains rolled up in west tower,
I'll see from hills come sudden shower.

Sima Guang (1019–1086)

EARLY SUMMER[1]

It turns fine after rain in fourth moon clear and clean;
The southern hills before my door are clearly seen.
With rising wind no riot will willow down run;
Only sunflowers turn their heads toward the sun.

---

[1] The poet describes early summer in four typical scenes: a fine day after vernal rain, a clear view of sunny hills, the falling willow down and the growing sunflowers.

Wang Anshi (1021–1086)

ON THE WINGED PEAK

On the Winged Peak a sky-scraping pagoda towers.
Cocks' crows are heard to wake sunrise at early hours.
Fear not the floating clouds may veil the sun from sight!
For you have placed yourself at the top of the height.

A Spring Night[1]

The incense burned away, the waterclock seems still;
The breeze blowing from time to time brings chill on chill.
How can I fall asleep when spring beauty's displayed:
Moonlight and flowers' shadows play on the balustrade?

---

[1] The poet was a prime minister who suffered setbacks in political
reform. This quatrain compares his setbacks to annoying spring and
he could only find comfort in the beauty of nature.

Moored at the Ferry

A river severs Northern shore and Southern land;
Between my home and me but a few mountains stand.
The vernal wind has greened the Southern shore again.
When will the moon shine bright on my return? O when?

SONG OF A RADIANT LADY[1]

When first the Radiant Lady left the palace, tears

Streamed down her vernal cheeks; locks hung limp o'er her ears.

Her face turned pale with lowered head and dreamy eyes;

Enchanted, the emperor could not hold back his sighs.

When she was gone, he blamed his first painter unfair,

Who made a picture untrue to a beauty rare.

He wrongly killed him for he knew nothing about

That no painter could bring a radiant beauty out.

She knew at heart she could never return, once gone;

Alas! Her robes brought from Han Palace were all outworn;

She longed to know what happened south of the frontier

And watched the message-bearing swans from year to year.

At last news came from home a thousand miles away:

"Don't think of us but stay in the tent as you may!"

Have you not seen

Another beauty locked in Palace Long Gate?

North and south, beauties out of favor share the same fate.

---

[1] The Radiant Lady whose beautiful face was not fairly portrayed by the first painter, was sent in 33 B.C. from the Palace of Han to marry the chieftain of the Tartars living in the tent.

THE LUNAR NEW YEAR'S DAY[①]

With crackers' cracking noise the old year passed away;
The vernal breeze brings us warm wine and warm spring day.
The rising sun sheds light on doors of each household,
New peachwood charm is put up to replace the old.

---

① It was believed in China that firecrackers' noise and peachwood charm
hung on the door could drive evil spirits away. So new peach wood
charm should be put up to replace the old on the lunar New Year's
Day. This quatrain was written when the poet was prime minister,
who believed his political reform would bring about changes for the
better just as the new charm would replace the old.

POOLSIDE APRICOT FLOWERS

The northern pool surrounds blooming apricot trees,
Their flowers and shadows bewitch the vernal day.
Although blown off like snowflakes by the vernal breeze,
They shame the petals ground to dust on southern way.

WRITTEN ON MY NEIGHBOR'S WALL[①]

No moss grows under your thatched eaves oft swept clean;
Flowers and trees you planted flank your pathway new.
Your fields are girded with a stream of water green;
Two high peaks towering in front exhale the blue.

---

① The poet who was once prime minister in the court writes this poem
when he lives in the countryside. This shows he knows what to do in
public life as well as in private life.

THE NORTHERN MOUNTAIN[①]

The lake overflows with northern mountain's green hue;
Straight canals shimmer with winding lake shores in view.
Counting the fallen petals, long I sit and wait.
Seeking for fragrant grass, slowly I come back late.

---

① The poet, when released from premiership, returned to the countryside
and wrote this quatrain, in which we find his love of nature and his
communion with it.

Zheng Xie (1022–1072)

AT THE END OF SPRING

When spring draws near its end, I sigh for home in vain;
The vernal wind should wonder why I'm far away.
I passed o'er mountain-tops by night and heard it rain;
I find the clear stream covered with petals by day.
At the turn of the road the trees are lost to sight;
No sooner left behind, the cloud has veiled the mountain.
The countryside of dirt and dust is often light;
I only see white sand steeped in transparent fountain.

Liu Ban (1023–1089)

THE FIRST FINE DAY AFTER RAIN

After the rain the day turns fine and moss turns green;
Awake from noonday dream, no men but trees are seen.
The south wind, old acquaintance, steals into my nook
And turns over the pages of my poetry book.

Wang Anguo (1028–1074)

PRINCE TENG'S PAVILION

Prince Teng was fond of visiting each pretty scene;
His lofty tower still o'er looks the river green.
The ups and downs of dynasties have come in view;
The setting sun slants, laden with griefs old and new.
The town is thick with trees that shade a thousand shops;
The horizon is dotted with a sail that flops.
Endlessly I sing of waves stretching out of sight
And watch o'er Western Hills cloud upon cloud in flight.

Wang Ling (1032–1059)

DROUGHT AND HEAT

The drought and heat last too long for fresh winds to kill;
The winged setting sun will not descend the hill.
The human world's afraid the seas and streams go dry;
Won't gods care for the Heavenly River on high?
Mount Kunlun, though steep, with perpetual snow is crowned;
The Fairy Isles, so far-off, in coolness is drowned.
Since I can't bring the world to enjoy their fresh breeze,
Could I go there alone to make a tour with ease?

WON'T SPRING COME BACK[1]

In late spring flowers fall but they will blow again,
And swallows come back under the eaves now and then.
At midnight cuckoos cry and ooze blood without cease;
They won't believe they can't call back the vernal breeze.

---

[1] The poet died at the age of twenty-eight, but he did not believe the blood-oozing cuckoo could not call back spring by its bloody songs. This quatrain seems to mean that the poet would revive by his verse.

Cheng Hao (1032–1085)

IMPROMPTU LINES ON A SPRING DAY

Towards noon 'neath fleecy clouds and gentle breeze
I cross the stream 'mid blooms and willow trees.
Some worldlings who don't know my heart's deep pleasure
Would say I'm like a truant fond of leisure.

WRITTEN AT RANDOM[1]

There's nothing I do but with ease when I'm at leisure;

Awake, I find east window reddened in sunlight.

Nature contemplated calmly has its own pleasure;

I enjoy four seasons with all men in delight.

Law is formless but reigns over heaven and earth;

Thoughts assume various shapes and change like wind and cloud,

Wealth can't seduce me; poverty won't reduce mirth.

A man who attains this of his deeds may be proud.

---

[1] This is a philosophical poem which tells us the importance of man's communion with nature, that is to say, a man should adapt his inner world to the outer world.

AN EXCURSION[1]

On fragrant grass in verdant plain I go as I will,

When spring has entered into green woods in far-off hill.

I see the reds run riot between willow trees;

When tired, I sit on riverside rock as I please.

Do not refuse to get drunk with a cup of wine.

I fear the wind would blow away all flowers fine.

The weather's clear and bright as on the Mourning Day.

Make a trip, but do not forget your homeward way!

---

[1] This poem shows the communion of man with nature on a vernal trip.

Cai Que (1037–1093)

A SUMMER DAY IN THE PAVILION[1]

On stone pillow in bamboo bed with paper screen,

Tired, I throw my book away and take a nap long.

Awake from dream, I rise and smile alone, unseen,

For I've heard on the waves the fisherman's flute song.

---

[1] The poet was prime minister under Emperor Xiao Zong of the Song. This quatrain shows how he spends his leisure when he is no longer Prime minister, and how much he loves a fisherman's carefree life.

Su Shi (1037–1101)

A POEM TO MY BROTHER ZIYOU, COMPOSED ON HORSEBACK AFTER PARTING WITH HIM AT THE WESTERN GATE OF THE CAPITAL ON THE NINETEENTH DAY OF THE ELEVENTH MOON[①]

Why do I look so drunken without drinking wine?

My heart is going back with your home-going steed.

Your thoughts turn to our parents and ancestral shrine.

How can I be consoled with the lonely life I'll lead?

Ascending a height, I look back and feel so sad

To see your black cap now appear, now disappear.

It is now biting cold and you are thinly clad,

Riding a lean nag 'neath the waning moon so drear.

Wayfarers sing abroad, people are glad at home,

My footman wonders why alone I'm desolate.

I know people may meet or part, settle down or roam,

But I dread to think how quickly years evaporate.

Facing a cold lamp, I relive the bygone days.

When may we listen to bleak wind on rainy night?

You know what I mean and must bear it in mind always:

Don't outstay your office of which you should make light!

---

① Having seen the poet on his way to Fengxiang, where he was to be assistant magistrate(in 1061), his brother started back.

VISITING IN WINTER THE TWO LEARNED MONKS IN THE LONELY HILL

It seems snowflake on flake
Will fall on cloudy lake;
Hills loom and fade, towers appear and disappear.
Fish can be count'd among the rocks in water clear;
Birds call back and forth in the deep woods men forsake.
I cannot go home on this lonely winter day,
So I visit the monks to while my time away.
Who can show me the way leading to their door-sill?
Follow the winding path to the foot of the hill.
The Lonely Hill is so lonesome. Who will dwell there?
Strong in faith, there's no loneliness but they can bear.
Paper windows keep them warm in bamboo cottage deep;
Sitting in their coarse robes, on round rush mats they sleep.
My lackeys grumble at cold weather and long road;
They hurry me to go before dusk to my abode.
Leaving the hill, I look back and see woods and cloud
Mingled and wild birds circling the pagoda proud.
This trip has not tired me but left an aftertaste;
Come back, I seem to see in dreams the scene retraced.
I hasten to write down in verse what I saw then,
For the scene lost to sight can't be revived again.

WRITTEN WHILE DRUNKEN IN LAKE VIEW PAVILION

Dark clouds like spilt ink spread over the mountains quiet;

Raindrops like bouncing pearls into the boat run riot.

A sudden rolling gale dispels clouds far and nigh;

Calmed water in the lake becomes one with the sky.

ON MY WAY TO NEW TOWN

The eastern wind foresees I will go to the wood;

It blows off endless songs sung by rain on the eaves.

The mountain's crowned with rainbow cloud like silken hood;

The rising sun like a brass gong hangs o'er the leaves.

Peach blossoms smile o'er the bamboo fence not tall;

Willow trees by the clear sand-paved brook sway and swing.

Folks in the Western Hills should be happiest of all;

They send well-cooked food to those who till in spring.

DRINKING AT THE LAKE, FIRST IN SUNNY, THEN IN RAINY WEATHER

The brimming waves delight the eye on sunny days;

The dimming hills present rare view in rainy haze.

West Lake may be compared to Lady of the West,[①]

Whether she is richly adorned or plainly dressed.

---

① Xi Shi (fl. 482 B.C.), a beautiful lady born near West Lake.

TWO LONELY ISLES IN THE YANGZI RIVER
WRITTEN ON A PICTURE DRAWN BY LI SIXUN

Below the mountains green
Water runs till unseen;
In the midst of the stream two lonely isles stand high.
Fallen crags bar the way;
Birds and apes cannot stay;
Only the giant trees tower into the sky.
From where comes a sail white?
In mid-stream rises oarsmen's undulating song.
Sand bar is flat, the wind is weak, no boat in sight,
The Lonely Isles sink and swim with the sail for long,
Like mist-veiled tresses of a pretty lass
Using the river as her looking glass.
O merchant in the boat, don't go mad for the fair!
The Lonely Isle and Gallant Hill are a well-matched pair.[1]

---

[1] The legend went that the God of Gallant Hill and the Goddess of the Lonely Isles were man and wife.

THE HUNDRED-PACE RAPIDS

Waves leap up where the long, long rapids steeply fall;
A light boat southwards shoots like plunging shuttle, lo!
Water birds fly up at the boatman's desperate call.
Among the rocks it strives to thread its way and go
As a hare darts away, an eagle dives below,
A gallant steed runs down a slope beyond control,
A string snaps from a lute, an arrow from a bow,
Lightning cleaves clouds or off lotus leaves raindrops roll.
The mountains whirl around, the wind sweeps by the ear,
I see the current boil in a thousand whirlpools.
At the risk of my life I feel a joy without peer,
Just like the god who boasts of the river he rules.[1]
Our life will pass like water running day and night;
Our thoughts can in a twinkling go beyond ninth sphere.[2]
Many people in drunken dreams contend and fight.
Do they know palaces 'mid weeds will disappear?
Awakened, they'd regret they've lost a thousand days;
Coming here, they will find the river freely rolls.

---

[1] According to Zhuang Zi, the River God boasted that the overflowing autumn river he ruled was without a peer.

[2] The ninth sphere was supposed to be the zenith of Heaven.

If on the riverside rocks you just turn your gaze,

You will find only honeycombs of the punt poles.

If your mind from earthly things is detached and freed,

Although nature may change, at ease you will remain.

Let us go back or in a boat or on a steed.

Our abbot will not like such an argument vain.

CRABAPPLE FLOWER[1]

The flower in east wind exhales a tender light,

And spreads a fragrant mist when the moon turns away.

I am afraid she'd fall asleep at dead of night,

A candle's lit to make her look fair as by day.

---

[1] Emperor Xuan Zong compared the drunken Lady Yang to a crabapple flower. Here the poet compares the flower to a sleepy beautiful lady. Both show their love of beauty.

WRITTEN ON THE WALL OF WEST FOREST TEMPLE[①]

It's a range viewed in face and peaks viewed from the side,
Assuming different shapes viewed from far and wide.
Of Mountain Lu we cannot make out the true face,
For we are lost in the heart of the very place.

———————————————

① In the third month of this year, the poet was ordered to more to
Ruzhou in Henan, an indication that his sentence had been lightened
and he was free to more beyond the confines of Huangzhou. Before
proceeding to Ruzhou, he crossed the Yangzi River and travelled south
to visit his brother.

VERNAL SCENE ON A RIVER

Beyond bamboos a few twigs of peach blossoms blow;
When spring has warmed the stream, ducks are the first to know.
By waterside short reeds bud and wild flowers teem;
It is just time for the globefish to swim upstream.

WINTER SCENE[1]

The lotus puts up no umbrella to the rain;
Yet frost-proof branches of chrysanthemums remain.
Do not forget of a year the loveliest scene
When oranges look like gold and tangerines jade-green.

---

[1] The poet is a broad-minded man who knows every season has its own beauty. In early winter when all flowers are fallen and mume blooms not yet in blossom, there are still golden oranges and tangerines, and the fruit is worth no less than the flower.

IMPROMPTU VERSE WRITTEN IN EXILE

I

Dishevelled white hair flows in the wind like frost spread;
In my small study I lie ill in wicker bed.
Knowing that I am sleeping a sweet sleep in spring, [1]
The Taoist priest takes care morning bells softly ring.

---

[1] The poet was exiled farther south for the 3rd line.

II

I, lonely Master of Eastern Slope, lie ill in bed;
My straggling white beard flows in the wind like frost spread.
Seeing my crimson face, my son is glad I'm fine;
I laugh, for he does not know I have drunken wine.

Huang Tingjian (1045–1105)

PARTING AT NIGHTFALL

Amid the farewell songs the river eastward flows;
By lamplight at the hillside my fishing boat goes.
I drink my fill till drunk as usual with glee;
But a streamful of breeze and moonlight grieves for me.

TO HUANG JIFU

I live in north and you in south, both by seaside;
I ask the swan to send you word but I'm denied.
A cup of wine beneath peach trees in vernal breeze;
Ten lonely years by the lamplight in rainy night.
In your home only stand four unfurnished walls;
To cure the State of ills you need no rise and falls.
I seem to see your white-haired head buried in books,
And hear the gibbons cry o'er the infected brooks.

THE FAIRY HILLS VIEWED IN RAIN FROM YUEYANG TOWER①

I

Having braved many dangers makes my hair turn grey;
Now I've survived in Three Gorges the deadly hour.
Before I reach my southern shore, I laugh so gay
To face the twelve Fairy Hills from the Yueyang Tower.

---

① Exiled in the west for five years, the poet, on his way to his native land in Jiangxi, passed the Three Gorges and Lake Dongting where was buried the queen of Emperor Shun or the Lady of River Xiang, whose spirit was said to dwell in the Fairy Hills.

II

Leaning alone on rails, I see the tempest break;

The twelve peaks stand like tresses of the Fairy Queen.

If I could view them from the overflowing lake,

I'd see 'mid mountain-high silver waves twelve hills green.

THE SOUTHERN TOWER[①]

Looking around, I find bright hills blend with rills bright;

Leaning on rails, I smell fragrance of lotus flower.

The breeze is free to blow and the moon to shed light;

They bring refreshing coolness to the Southern Tower.

---

① This quatrain describes the poet as free to enjoy the coolness of summer
and beauty of nature as the breeze to blow and the moon to shed light.

TWO QUATRAINS IN REPLY TO LI HEFU

I

The mountains look serene as the song of the stream;
I roll up window-screen to see the bright moonbeam.
I hear a plaintive flute from the twin boats arise;
It tells my friend's regret and sighs his far-off sighs.

II

The bygone days come at my will into my dream;
For drunken eyes past splendor in a mess would seem.
Troubled that I cannot set my ideal apart,
I wish that I were born with an unfeeling heart.

A PICTURE OF FAREWELL

I

After heart-broken songs the wayfarer's unseen;
The silent picture presents a heart-breaking scene.
What will he see on his way west of Sunny Pass?
Only the cattle when north wind blows down the grass.

II

Of all the human griefs the parting one lasts long;
Longmian makes a picture of the heart-breaking song.
The tavern willow has nothing to gnaw its heart;
'Tis the grief of those who are unwilling to part.

Qin Guan (1049–1100)

EVENING VIEW FROM SIZHOU[①]

The lonely town is girt by a long river white
Patched with happy fore-and-aft sails in twilight.
In a stretch of picturesque blue the forest's drowned;
It should be the hills where the River Huai turns round.

---

① Sizhou was a lonely town situated on the River Huai and now sunk in
the Lake Hongze.

Chen Shidao (1053–1102)

THE TIDAL BORE VIEWED ON THE SEVENTEENTH DAY OF THE EIGHTH MOON

White rainbows run riot on vast expanse of sand;
Numerous silver cups fall from immortals' hand.
The azure sky's convulsed in its watery graves;
The setting sun sinks or swims with turbulent waves.

Zhang Lei (1054–1114)

SUMMER DAYS[1]

By riverside summer days are long with breeze light,
Under the eaves young swallows and sparrows in flight.
Butterflies bask and dance at noon on blooming trees;
A spider weaves its web in a corner with ease.
The moon embroiders shadows on my window screen;
My pillow inhales the murmuring stream unseen.
The hair on my forehead has tamed snow-white for long;
I'd pass my life enjoying a fisherman's song.

---

[1] The poet can write at thirteen. This poem shows his love for rural life.

AT FIRST SIGHT OF MOUNT SONG

Tired for years of the dust raised by steeds on my way,
My mind is only eased at sight of mountains green.
At dusk the northern wind has blown the rain away;
Out of the clouds emerge rocky peaks steep and lean.

Chao Yuezhi (1059–1129)

PICTURE OF BALL PLAYING[1]

See thousands of palace gates open one and all:
The emperor comes back drunk after playing ball.
The loyal ministers are old or die of sorrow;
No one would venture an admonition tomorrow.

---

[1] This is a satire against Emperor Xuan Zong of the Tang Dynasty, who neglected his duty for drinking and playing ball with his favorite lady.

Cowherd

A COWHERD'S SONG[1]

Grass overgrows for miles and miles across the plain;
I play on flute in evening breeze thrice and again.
Come back, I eat my fill at the fall of the night,
Without doffing my straw cloak, I lie in moonlight.

---

[1] The poet writes in the person of a cowherd. This quatrain shows his love of pastoral life. Whether he is noble or humble, a man may find pleasure in communion with nature. That is the reason why ancient intelligent men made light of wealth and fame in the world.

Monk Huihong (1071–1128)

THE SWING①

Between two painted posts hangs an emerald swing;
A maiden plays on it before the bower in spring.
Her trailing crimson skirt above the ground goes high;
Her pretty looks are welcome even in the sky.
Apricot reddens her seat like rain in the breeze;
The colored ropes hang under smokelike willow trees.
Getting down from the swing, she stands at leisure soon,
As if she were a fairy come down from the moon.

---

① This is a picture of a fair maiden on the swing.

Xu Fu (1075–1141)

A SPRING DAY ON THE LAKE

When will the swallows pair by pair fly back again?
Peach blossoms on both shores just above water float.
I cannot cross the bridge submerged by vernal rain.
What joy to see from willow shade come out a boat!

Li Gang

TO A SICK BUFFALO

You've ploughed field on field and reaped crop on crop of grain.
Who would pity you when you are tired out and done?
If old and young could eat their fill, then you would fain
Exhaust yourself and lie sick in the setting sun.

Li Qingzhao (1084–1151)

A QUATRAIN

Be man of men while you're alive;
Be soul of souls e'en though you're dead!
Think of Xiang Yu[1] who'd not survive
His men, whose blood for him was shed.

---

[1] Xiang Yu (232-202 B.C.), who, defeated by Liu Bang, first emperor of the Han Dynasty, killed himself beside the Black River after singing his last song.

Zeng Ji (1084–1166)

ON MY WAY IN THE MOUNTAINS[①]

When mume fruit turns yellow, it's fine from day to day;
Leaving the stream, in the mountains I go my way.
I find the shade as green as when I came alone;
What is more, I hear four or five golden orioles' song.

---

① This quatrain describes the pleasure of sunny days in a rainy season. The
poet enjoys the beauty of nature while travelling on water or on land.

Chen Yuyi (1090–1138)

THE CHILL OF SPRING

From day to day the wind blows in the second moon;
In the lingering cold I worry for the flowers.
The crab apple reveals her rouged cheeks alone,
Careless alike of drizzling rain and drenching showers.

Zhu Shuzhen

THE SCENE IN VIEW[1]

My lonely window shaded by swaying bamboo,

At sunset I hear lovebirds chirping two by two.

Crabapple flowers fade, willow down flies away.

What drowsy weather when begins the lengthening day!

---

[1] The poetess describes how she passes the drowsy day in the shade of green bamboos amid the songs of lovebirds while she regrets faded crabapple flowers and fallen willow down.

FALLEN FLOWERS[1]

Flowers are blooming on entwined branches by the wall,

But jealous wind and rain would hasten them to fall.

If the Vernal God should reign as the floral boss,

Let no petals fall in showers over green moss!

---

[1] The poetess compares a couple of lovers to the entwined branches of a tree, and their separation to the fallen flowers. The wind and rain are personified to hasten their separation. This is a symbolic poem.

Lu You (1125–1210)

INDIGNATION

How could I know the hard times in my early days?
Looking north, I heave up and down like mountain ways.
Warships crossed Melon Ferry on a snowy night;
Armored steeds ran in autumn breeze to border height.
In vain I'd be a "Great Wall" to bar the foe's way;
Before its time my hair in the mirror turns grey.
The premier's fame is widespread even on frontiers.
Who can boast to equal him for a thousand years?

A SUNNY SPRING DAY AFTER A RAINY NIGHT IN THE CAPITAL

The world tastes chilly like thin gauze in recent years.
Who tells you to ride in the capital like Peers?
Last night in the attic I heard the vernal rain;
Next day apricot blooms will be sold in deep lane.
On short paper I try my calligraphy free;
Under the window I enjoy my bubbled tea.
Do not complain your white dress is soiled in the breeze!
You may go home before Mourning Day if you please.

EARLY DAWN AT MY WICKET GATE

The long, long River flows eastward into the sea;
The high, high Mountains looking upward scrape the sky.
The refugees have shed all their tears in debris;
Another year will pass, no royal army's nigh.

THE STORM ON THE FOURTH DAY OF THE ELEVENTH MOON

Forlorn in a cold bed, I'm grieved not for my plight,
Still thinking of recovering our lost frontiers.
Hearing the stormy wind and rain at dead of night,
I dreamed of frozen rivers crossed by cavaliers.

THE GARDEN OF SHEN[①]

I

The horn blows sad at sunset on the city wall;
In garden of old days I find no poolside hall.
To see the green waves beneath the bridge would break my heart,
For they have seen your swanlike shadow come and part.

II

Your fragrance has not sweetened my dreams for forty years;
The willows grow so old that no catkin appears.
I'll soon become a clod of clay beneath the hill;
Again I come in tears to find your traces still.

---

① In the Garden of Shen the poet met with his first wife, Tan Wan, whom he loved dearly, yet was compelled to divorce. They wrote two lyrics to the tune of "Phoenix Hairpin" in 1155. In 1200 the poet revisited the garden alone and wrote these two poems.

A QUATRAIN ON MUME BLOSSOMS

'Tis said against cold morning wind mume blossoms blow
All over four mountains like pile on pile of snow.
Could I be multiplied into ten thousand me,
You would find my person before every mume tree.

TESTAMENT TO MY SON

After my death I know for me all hopes are vain,
But still I'm grieved to see our country not unite.
When Royal Armies recover the Central Plain,
Do not forget to tell your Sire in sacred rite!

Fan Chengda (1126–1193)

The Lakeside Lane

Spring has come and greened all over the southern land;
The stone bridge and red tower face to face still stand.
From year to year friends are seen off on Lakeside Lane;
The weeping willow would tie their boat in fine rain.

Rural Life

I Spring

The fertile soil is unfroze by frequent rain;
Grasses grow lush and flowers burst forth one and all.
The waste garden behind my house turns green again;
My neighbor's bamboo stem shoots out from under the wall.

II Summer

Our sons go out to cultivate the fields by day;
By night our daughters weave thread into cloth with ease.
Their children cannot help their parents, so they stay
And learn to sow melon seed 'neath mulberry trees.

III AUTUMN

Flat as a mirror our newly-built threshing ground,

House on house beats the grain after frost on days bright.

In our laughter and song e'en thunder would be drowned;

We wield the flail pitter-patter all through the night.

You Mao (1127–1194)

RIVER XIAO XIANG WRITTEN ON A PICTURE DRAWN BY MI YUANHUI

I

The river mingles with the sky;

In misty village trees stand high.

Listening to rain in a boat,

On the Xiao Xiang I'd seem to float.

II

The hills are barred with cloud in dream;

A stretch of sand borders the stream.

In fisherman's green cloak I'd go

And float my cot there to and fro.

Yang Wanli (1127—1206)

GRIEF IN SPRING[1]

I thought this spring would bring more pleasure than before,
But I've enjoyed the eastern breeze and nothing more.
From year to year I have no eyes to enjoy flowers,
For I am laden with grief or ill in my bowers.

---

[1] The poet is the compiler of this book in Chinese. This quatrain makes a contrast between the poor peasants who have to till the ground and gather mulberry leaves by day and feed silk worms and weave cloth by night till the cuckoos sing at daybreak, with the rich ladies who dance or make merry all night long.

AFTER A NAP IN EARLY SUMMER[1]

The juice of mume makes my teeth feel a sourness keen;
Banana leaves share their green with my window screen.
What at after a long day nap can I do with pleasure?
I only watch the kids catch willow down at leisure.

---

[1] This quatrain describes four scenes typical of early summer: drinking of mume juice, taking a long noonday nap, enjoying the green shade of banana leaves and seeing the willow down flying away.

THE WEST LAKE

The uncommon West Lake in the midst of sixth moon
Displays a scenery to other months unknown;
Green lotus leaves outspread as far as boundless sky;
Pink lotus blossoms take from sunshine a new dye.

PASSING BY SONGYUAN

Don't say downhill no obstacles before you lie,
Misleading wayfarers to be happy and gay!
You are surrounded by ten thousand mountains high:
One mountain lets you pass, another bars your way.

Lin Sheng

WRITTEN AT THE NEW CAPITAL

Hills rise beyond blue hills; towers beyond high towers.

When will West Lake end its singing and dancing hours?

The revelers are drunk with vernal breeze and leisure;

They'd seek in the new capital for their lost pleasure.

Zhu Xi (1130–1200)

A SPRING DAY[1]

I seek for spring by riverside on a fine day,

O what refreshing sight does the boundless view bring?

I find the face of vernal wind in easy way:

Myriads of reds and violets reveal only spring.

---

[1] This quatrain shows that the invisible spring can be seen in myriads of reds and violets. Delight in life is the essence of Confucian wisdom.

THE BOOK[1]

There lies a glassy oblong pool,

Where light and shade pursue their course.

How can it be so clear and cool?

For water fresh comes from its source.

---

[1] The book is compared to a clear pool.

THE FLOATING SHIP[1]

The vernal water rose by riverside last night;

A stranded heavy ship became a feather light.

Before the flood all effort's vain to push it go;

Now with ease it may move in midstream to and fro.

---

[1] This is another symbolic quatrain in which the poet compares man to a
ship and knowledge to water. A heavy ship cannot float on shallow but on
deep water, nor can a man fulfill a heavy duty without deep knowledge.

POMEGRANATE FLOWERS[1]

Pomegranates in the fifth moon dazzle the sight;

Among the branches you perceive their seeds pearl-bright.

But this is a place where no cabs nor horses cross;

You see only reds fallen pell-mell on green moss.

---

[1] This is a picture of summer in the fifth moon when pomegranate flowers blow unenjoyed in a deserted place. The poet seems to mean that a man should choose the right place to do the right thing.

Monk Zhinan

A QUATRAIN[1]

I moor my small boat in the shade of ancient trees,

Crossing the bridge, cane in hand, I go where I please.

The drizzle moistens my gown with wet apricot,

The wind caressing my face with willows chills me not.

---

[1] The poet is not displeased with chilling wind and rain, in boat or on shore. This shows his love of nature and even his communion with it.

Zhang Shi (1133–1180)

IMPROMPTU LINES WRITTEN ON THE SPRING DAY[1]

Warmth comes late in the year, ice and frost disappear;
When spring returns on earth, grass and woods feel the mirth.
Everything comes to life again before my eyes;
The east wind blows, I see green ripples fall and rise.

---

[1] The Spring Day falls a few days after the lunar New Year's Day to mark the beginning of the season. This quatrain describes the beauty of nature and implies its communion with man.

Weng Juan

RURAL LIFE[1]

All hills and fields are clad in green and streams in white;
Cuckoos shed tears while rain drizzles like vapor light.
The peasants in the fourth moon are busy farm hand;
Having just fed the silkworms, they should till the land.

---

[1] This is a picture of rural life in the fourth moon, in which the poet describes not only the peasants but also the green hills where they have planted mulberry trees to feed silkworms, the green fields they have tilled, the white water they use to irrigate the fields and even the cuckoos which would add a few tears to the irrigation. This shows the harmony between man and nature.

Zhao Shixiu (1170–1219)

A PROMISE UNKEPT[1]

In rainy season house on house is steeped in rain;
On poolside meadow here and there frogs croak in vain.
My friend's not kept his word to come, now it's midnight.
What can I do but play chess alone by lamplight?

---

[1] Early summer is a long rainy season when the fruit will turn yellow on
mume trees. This quatrain describes how the poet spends a rainy night
without a companion.

Dai Fugu (1167–1252)

A PLEASURE GARDEN IN EARLY SUMMER[1]

Nursling ducks swim in pools deep here and shallow there;
Mume fruit is ripe, the weather now cloudy now fair.
I bring wine to drink in the garden east and west,
And strip the loquat of golden fruit without rest.

---

[1] This quatrain describes the poet making merry at a time neither fine nor
rainy, in a place where water is deep here and shallow there. This shows
the poet knows how to choose the golden mean.

Gao Zhu (1170–1241)

THE MOURNING DAY[1]

There're many graveyards in northern and southern hill;
On Mourning Day the mourners come and weep their fill.
Burnt paper money flies as white as butterflies;
The bloodlike tears are shed and dye azaleas red.
At sunset foxes come back to lie there at night;
At home the mourners would laugh by the candlelight.
While he is alive, a man should in wine be drowned.
When dead, could he drink a drop of wine underground?

---

[1] The previous poem says sage or fool must die one day or another; this poem says it would be better to drink and make merry while one may. Such was the attitude towards life of many intellectuals.

Liu Kezhuang (1187–1269)

THE SHUTTLING ORIOLES[1]

So deep in love, you shuttle between willow trees;
You twitter when you play with the loom as you please.
The blooming capital in spring looks like brocade,
With how much labor is the woven picture made?

---

[1] The poet compares the oriole to a shuttle and the garden to a loom. The oriole flies among the trees as swiftly as a shuttle passes in the loom, to weave a picture of spring. The oriole is personified to symbolize the laborers who have built the brocadelike capital.

Ye Shaoweng (fl.1224)

CALLING ON A FRIEND WITHOUT MEETING HIM

How could the green moss like my sabots, whose teeth[1] sting?
I tap long at the door, but none opens at my call.
The garden can't confine the full beauty of spring;
An apricot extends a blooming branch o'er the wall.

---

[1] Chinese sabots had teeth.

Zheng Hui

WRITTEN ON THE WALL OF AN INN[1]

She shivers with spring cold in her flower-sweetened dream,
Double doors veiled in green, swallows perch on the beam,
Trimming the candle by taking off her hairpin,
She may anticipate I'm lodging at the inn.

---

[1] This quatrain describes the poet's nostalgia on his way home, by imagining his wife's longing for his return.

Bai Yuchan (1194–?)

EARLY SPRING[1]

On sunny branches two or three mumes begin to blow;
I like their fragrance and petals powdered with snow.
Pale in mist and silver in moonlight they stand;
They blush in water deep and smile on shallow sand.

---

[1] The poet is a Taoist priest. This quatrain shows his love of mume blossoms powdered with snow and steeped in moonlight. This proves he is cold-proof as the flower, pure as snow and clear as the moon.

Wang Qi

VISITING A SMALL GARDEN IN LATE SPRING^①

Since the mume blossom takes off her rosy attire,
The crabapple has rouged her face as red as fire.
When roseleaf raspberry fades, comes the end of flowers all;
Only the trailing plants appear over the mossy wall.

---

① The poet describes late spring by three flowers which fade one after another, but he advises us not to grieve over its departure, for when all flowers fade, life will reappear in trailing plants and green moss.

MUME BLOSSOMS^①

No dust has left the least stain on the pure mume flower;
She is content with bamboo fence and thatched bower.
But married by mistake to the poet of crane,
She is glorified in verse again and again.

---

① A hermit living in the Lonely Hill said that he would have the mume flower as his wife and the crane as his son. This quatrain glorifies the purity of the flower as well as of the hermit or poet of crane, though humorously.

Lei Zhen

RURAL SCENE AT DUSK[①]

Green grass overgrows the shore of the brimming pool;
The sun pecked by hills sinks into ripples cool.
A cowherd comes back astride on a buffalo;
He blows on his short flute a tune he may not know.

---

① This is a picture of sunset between two hills reflected on water. The
cowherd coming back for rest is just like the sun going down for rest
too. There is harmony between man and nature.

Lu Meipo

MUME AND SNOW

I

The mume blossoms and snow vie in announcing spring;
A poet knows not in whose praises he should sing.
The mume blossoms are not so white as winter snow;
In fragrance snow can't match mume blossoms when they blow.

Wen Tianxiang (1236–1283)

SAILING ON LONELY OCEAN[1]

Delving in "the Book of Change," I rose through hardship great
And desperately fought the foe for four long years.
Like willow down the war-torn land looks desolate;
I sink or swim as duckweed in the rain appears.
For the perils on Perilous Beach I heaved sighs;
On Lonely Ocean now I feel dreary and lonely.
Since olden days there's never been a man but dies;
I'd leave a loyalist's name in history only.

---

[1] Wen Tianxiang passed the civil service examinations with highest honors in 1256 and was appointed prime minister in the court of the Song Dynasty. In 1275 he led the royalist army against the Tartar invaders. Defeated, he passed Perilous Beach in 1276. Captured in 1278, he passed Lonely Ocean, a part of the South China Sea.

PASSING THE POST AT JINLING①

The setting sun will leave the place o'ergrown with grass.

A lonely drifting cloud, to whom can I adhere?

The mountains and the rivers seem the same, alas!

But half our towns are lost, half our men disappear.

Reed catkins will turn grey as grey will grow my head.

Into whose house will swallows of old mansions fly?

On Southern shore from now on I'll no longer tread,

But I'll come back with blood oozing in cuckoo's cry.

---

① Wen Tianxiang was captured by the Tartar aggressors in 1278 and sent to Yanjing (modern Beijing). He met with a friend at the post of Jinling (modern Nanjing) and wrote the above poem.

Yuan Dynasty
(1271–1368)

Hao Jing (1223—1275)

FALLEN FLOWERS

As rainbow clouds o'er darkened door, red petals shower;

On jadeite branch is left the trace of fallen flower.

Of peach and plum in eastern breeze dream butterflies;

For moonlit hills and northern walls cuckoo's soul cries.

Jade railings stand in chilly mist amid bare trees;

The beautygone in Golden Val, wine cups displease.

Don't sweep the blooms spread pell-mell in the yard away!

Let vernal beauty stay till the end of the day!

---

① This was written when the poet was detained in the south, so he compared himself to the butterfly and the cuckoo longing for the north.

② The beautiful Lady Green Pearl fell down from the tower in the Garden of Golden Val like fallen flowers in 300.

Chen Fu (1240–1303)

THE HAMMER BLOW[1]

How brave to strike at royal cab with hammer blow!
The empire, tottering, began to be brought low.
Though out of molten iron were made statues grand,
The hammer still was made by the rebellious hand.

---

[1] In 218 BC Zhang Liang tried to kill by hammer blow the first
emperor of Qin, who had molten iron weapons into twelve statues for
fear that they might be used by rebels.

SNOW ON THE RIVER AT DUSK

Jade flowers whirl in endless sky;
Sand islets whiten far and nigh.
No traces of wild geese withdrawn,
Cliffs loom at dusk as if at dawn.
The fisherman, cold, will go back,
But he has lost the beaten track.
His boat drifts while he sits asleep;
His cloak melts in mist dense and deep.

TO THE TEMPLE OF GOLDEN HILL

Bowing, you drink on boundless waves celestial light;
There is another heaven and earth on your height.
In your pagoda's shade cloud-veiled river's mouth hides;
Your ringing bells cross the sea gate with rising tides.
Your monk's cells tremble when the mermaids sink or swim;
Like castles in the air your Buddhist lamps look dim.
Only the water of your Central Fountain clear,
Remains without a stain or dust from year to year.

THE MOUNTAIN PASS

Like sharp swords broken cliffs stand ten thousand feet high;
O'er mossy rocks torn asunder no birds dare fly.
Old trees have no green branch in mountains high and low;
Though summer's at its height, in haste comes winter snow.
The way beyond the Pass with endless sand turns cold;
When camels growl at night, the yellow cloud grows old.
When wild geese cry in boundless sky o'er the Great Wall,
The breezes blow, the grass bends low, the moon seems small.

Dai Biaoyuan (1244–1310)

A SONGSTER ON WEST LAKE[1]

Peonies pink or violet embellish spring;

Beside the music score lie clappers with red string.

A white-haired man with cup of wine on southern shore,

Nobody knows he was the songster all adore.

---

[1] After the downfall of the Southern Song Dynasty, the poet regretted that the famous songster became unknown even on West Lake.

Liu Yin (1249–1293)

SONG OF THE WHITE WILD GEESE[1]

When the north wind first rose, the Northern Stream was chilled;

The second time it rose, the South with cold was filled.

The third time when it blew, white wild geese flew away;

The southernmost frontier grew cold, they could not stay.

The vernal breeze blew hot and cold three hundred years;

When the north wind sweeps o'er the land, it disappears.

For miles and miles on streams I think of freedom's reign

And wait for spring and wild geese to come back again.

---

[1] The north wind symbolizes the Tartar invaders, and the wild geese the loyalist of the Song Dynasty, and the vernal breeze and freedom refers to the Song Dynasty's reign.

MOUNTAINSIDE COTTAGE

Crossing the brook, my horse's hoofs disturb clouds bright[1];
Drunk, my sleeves flap with falling petals in breeze light.
I wonder how the lad knows my coming and wait;
The magpie's song arrives before me to his gate[2].

---

[1] The reflection of the clouds in the brook.
[2] The magpie's song was believed in ancient China to announce a good
news or the arrival of a guest.

ON SEEING THE MUME FLOWER[1]

The east wind blows up war dust and sand more and more;
I dream of mume-bloom-lover in his lakeside bower.
Spring beauty wanes, I fear, on southern rivershore;
My heart longs for the poet more than for the flower.

---

[1] Written after the downfall of the Southern Song capital where lived Lin
Bu (967–1028), the mume-loving poet of the Northern Song Dynasty.

A Moonlit Night in the Mountains

So full of gloomy thoughts, I'm desolate and drear;
At dead of night I face the empty mountains high.

The cliffs are whitened by the frost of autumn clear;
The moon emerges above the clouds flooding the sky.

The rocky valley echoes with my stirring strain;
My shadow trembles in the stream studd'd with starlight.

Drunken, I seem to hear the ape say to the crane:
For hundred years the world's not so fair as tonight!

Zhao Mengfu (1254–1322)

THE TOMB OF GENERAL YUE FEI[①]

The tomb of General Yue with grass is desolate;
In dreary autumn day the stone beasts stand like crags.
The rulers fleeing south made light of northern state;
People in Central Plain longed for the general's flags.
What is the use of regretting the hero's death?
How could half of the divided country last long?
Do not sing to West Lake this strain and waste your breath!
Hills mirrored in the waves can't bear your grievous song.

---

① General Yue Fei (1103–1141) who tried to recover the lost Central Plain
was sentenced to death by the emperor fleeing to the south and was
buried by the side of West Lake.

SPRING GRIEF

I close the double door when spring is drear and chill;
The incense burned, the golden censer is warm still.
The swallows will not come when again fall the flowers;
The courtyard thick with dusk is full of wind and showers.

AN EXCURSION RECALLED

On southern shore in late spring orioles flew in riot;

Hundreds of flowers bade adieu to willows quiet.

The fallen reds and songstress' fans bewitched the eye;

The envious tender green for dancer's robe would sigh.

In golden censer incense burned on stream at night,

My pleasure boat 'mid drumbeats came back by moonlight.

But now I'm solitary in the eastern breeze,

Wine cup in hand at sunset, silent, ill at ease.

A QUATRAIN

Moonlight on rivulet looks white as sand;

By riverside ten thousand houses stand.

Who plays on flute of jade when night is long?

A broken heart can't bear heart-breaking song.[1]

---

① The heart-breaking song refers to the "Blooming Jade Trees" composed by the last emperor (553–604) of the Chen Dynasty, whose capital of ten thousand houses was captured by the foe while he was playing a flute of jade on a moonlit night in 589.

Yang Zai (1271–1323)

THE MOON VIEWED FROM THE TAOIST HALL[1]

The Taoist Hall is water-chilly with moonlight;

I sit and watch the icy moon until midnight.

Like shadows looms the land with hills and rills in view;

From the Ninth Heaven fall the silent breeze and dew,

A pair of dragons bear the board with gold inlaid;

Two flying phoenixes play on the flute of jade.

How could I cross the sea of thirty thousand miles

To carry my body tonight to Fairy Islets?

---

[1] There was an inscribed board hanging high in the Taoist Hall.

WRITTEN IN THE LAKESIDE PAVILION[1]

The white birds fly in twos and threes;

Sideways they go where'er they please.

Hick clouds won't scatter after rain,

But hug the verdant hillside plain.

---

[1] The poet lived by the lakeside.

IN THE CAPITAL

When snow begins to melt in town, shepherd's purses grow;
At my side door in narrow lane few come and go.
On willow-tips I hear the golden orioles sing:
This is the first song that announces coming spring.

LATE SPRING ON NORTHERN HILLS BY WEST LAKE

I cling to listen to the rain with ears annoyed;
A beauty-lover fears northern hills unenjoyed.
How can I leave their flowers blossom in full bloom?
I'm glad to see a fine day vague in water loom.
Though tired, how can I not visit the temple hall?
Secluded, I won't go back to the city wall.
Green mulberries and wheat girt with cherries appear;
I then remember I have left home for a year.

Fan Peng (1272–1330)

LEAVING YANGZHOU

My lonely sail is passing round the sandy bar;
The lake is green with lotus leaves without pink blooms.
I turn my head to find the west Pavilion far;
On mist-and-rain-veiled stream a wine-shop streamer looms.

SONG OF GRAVE-DIGGING

The old grave dug out yesterday,
The new grave is dug right away.
Two graveside statues bid adieu
To the old and welcome the new.
The old soul not yet gone, the new one comes in deep;
Before the new comes, the old would bitterly weep.
The old soul tells the new one again and again:
You need not many offsprings if graves good remain.
If your offsprings unceasingly come one by one,
Your grave will be dug out one day by your grandson.
It is sad for my grave today to be dug out.
I know not when it's your turn to complain about.

Yu Ji (1272–1348)

SONG OF WHITE-PLUMED SKYLARKS

The white-plumed skylarks' neath Mongolian city wall,

Male and female, delight in hearing mutual call.

In desert there's no tree for them to build their nest;

'Mid withered grass beneath eighth moon's deep snow they rest.

Have you not seen

The Flying Swallow[1] in Sunny Palace of yore

And many love-birds locked up within somber door?

They heard dew drip on lotus each cold autumn night

And saw the breeze caress peonies in spring bright.

---

[1] The Flying Swallow was the favorite mistress of Emperor Cheng of the Han Dynasty in the first century BC.

SITTING ALONE IN THE COURTYARD

Where shall I find in future years the land of dreams?

Can I forget my native hills and Southern streams?

Why, standing round my house, should the moaning pine-trees

Remind me of the Southern rain when blows the breeze?

Elegy on Premier Wen Tianxiang[1]

In vain you wielded spear to raise the setting sun.

How could a Southern captive stop the north wind's run!

The hammer blow could not revenge the conquered State.

How could the premier change the Western Kingdom's fate!

Frow cloudy Tripod Lake the dragon's[2] far away.

On moonlit pillar could the immortal crane stay?

Why should we northward gaze again from Southern Tower?

Where on the conquered Southern shore can our tears shower!

---

[1] Wen Tianxiang (1232–1286), last premier of the Southern Song Dynasty, was captured by the Yuan army and executed.

[2] The sun and the dragon refer to the last emperor of the Song Dynasty, and the crane to Wen Tianxiang's soul.

ON COLD FOOD DAY[1]

The land is not mine though beautiful it appears;
My father and myself have roamed a hundred years.

By waterside their cottages stand and graveyard lies.
How can I bear to hear cuckoo's home-going cries![2]

---

[1] On Cold Food Day the Chinese people used to visit their ancestral graveyard and take cold meals.

[2] The cuckoo seems to sing in Chinese: "Why not go home?"

TO HISTORIAN YUAN IN IMPERIAL TRAIN[1]

The golden sunlight makes imperial robe more red;
In royal progress His Majesty rides ahead.

At dawn the steep sky-scraping path retains the cars;
At night the guards with bows stand round the tents like stars.

White steeds with broidered saddles bear the ladies fair,
And violet camels carry grapes in silver ware.

The followers in royal train come like rain-cloud;
Only Historian Yuan of talent can be proud.

---

[1] Each year Kubla Khan made a progress to the former capital where he mounted on throne.

Sa Dula (1272–?)

SONG OF A NORTHERN BEAUTY

The Northern beauty is sixteen,

With rosy face and eyebrows green.

The road is fragrant with her steed;

Short whip in hand, she rides with speed.

In vernal breeze vernal heart swings;

In candle-lit hall no lute sings.

Her broidered quilt can't warm her dreams;

'Neath misty sky no curtain gleams.

Years pass like water, who would care?

She is too tired to comb her hair.

Last night the streets were wet with rain;

The willow down[1] can't waft again.

---

① The willow down symbolizes the northern beauty.

SONG OF LOTUS FLOWER

The lotus flowers sweeten boundless autumn lake;
The heart of maiden fair by waterside would break.
Her rosy robe can't screen and warm the cloud-like flowers;
Her green sleeves are chilled by the wind in evening hours.
The carp raise waves and breakers whiten in the breeze;
Frost falls on Dongting Lake with dead leaves from the trees.
Where is the lotus-gatherer rowing her boat?
Could she forget the beautiful lotus afloat?

FRONTIER SONGS

I

At sunset here and there disperse cattle and sheep;
The cheese is all the sweeter mingled with grass's scent.
The sand flies up like snow when gales of north wind sweep;
All the felt curtains are let down from tent to tent.

II

It's hard to bend the bow in high wind at Great Wall,
But the young lords on hunting ground ride left and right.
Arrow at waist, they come back late with hawks they call,
On both sides of the saddle hanging two wolves white.

The Lady of Stone[1]

Alone by riverside precarious she appears;

No one accompanies her but songs water sings.

The hair on her forehead uncombed for thousand years,

Her beauty remains unchanged for as many springs.

The gentle wind spreads snowflakes to powder her face;

The sun will rouge her cheeks by melting dewdrops bright.

Don't say there is no mirror to reflect her grace!

The moon will shine on the Lady of Stone all night.

---

[1] According to a Chinese legend, a lady waiting for the return of her lord by the riverside turned into a statue and was called the Lady of Stone.

Jie Xisi (1274–1344)

BOATING IN SUMMER

Two bearded men, each with an oar, back to back row;
Their short straw cloaks in wind and rain up and down flow.
Blue mountains stretch like dragons far into the cloud;
Who are the white-haired men on sand-shore talking loud?
The boatmen fore and aft sing their song and refrain;
Below the awning I sit and listen to rain.
Pushing it aside, I do not know where am I;
What do I see but white gulls in pairs passing by?

A MOONLIT NIGHT

I

The rising moon shines o'er my garden deep;
My merry-making neighbors cannot sleep.
I shiver not with cold dew nor cold breeze;
But watch the moon grow round o'er shady trees.

II

When clear's the sky, nearer it seems to stay;
When night is deep, it sinks farther away.
East of my garden wall two poplars long;
Fill lonely room with lonely autumn song.

ON LEAVING WUCHANG[1]

On going home, none will delay;
But I dislike to start my way.
I long for home when the year ends;
Staying abroad long, I've new friends.
Standing, I gaze on river's flow;
And see the waves but homeward go.

---

[1] On going homeward towards Fengcheng in Jiangxi, the poet was
reluctant to leave his new friends in Wuchang.

COLD NIGHT

In frosty sky a few stars freeze;
Moonlight wets grass around the trees.
I cannot sleep in empty hall;
Now and then I hear a leaf fall.

ON RIVER GAN[1]

The islets with green grass o'erspread;

In wind and rain homeward I speed.

My ship in mid-stream sails ahead;

Blue mountains on both sides recede.

O'er Wood God's Temple crows raise cries;

To River God sacrifice's made.

The waves vie in dance, fall and rise;

O how much hardship we have paid!

---

[1] The poet sailed from Ji'an to Fengcheng in 1320 after having suffered much in life.

Zhang Yu (1277–1348)

BAMBOO BRANCH SONG[1]

Before the lake's the little cottage where I stay.

Will you please come, when you have leisure, to take tea?

My house is built of thatched roof and walls of clay;

In front of my door stands a blooming redbud tree.

---

[1] This is the imitation of a song composed by a Southern lass for a young man she loved.

Guan Yunshi (1286–1324)

A QUILT OF REED CATKINS

The reed catkins you have gathered from dust are clean;

They're used to fill my quilt or paddled straw cloak green.

In boundless autumn my dream wafts as west winds blow;

The moon sheds fragrance and I seem covered with snow.

My hair and hones grow old with the earth and the sky;

My fame won't yield to ancient or modern sages high.

Don't envy silken quilt on which the love birds sing!

In a fisherman's song there is another spring.

PEACH BLOSSOM MOUNTAIN①

Three thousand years have passed since left the beauty bright;

I long for him as if he were in front of me.

Peach blossoms redden rain and fall on Mountain White;

I know from human world the immortal would flee.

The empty mountain towers by night as by day;

Old trees cry and exhale sad cloud in crimson dyed.

How's the mountain transformed where immortals would stay?

For miles and miles cloud and mist hang by riverside.

Spring comes to life when fragrance spreads from mountains proud;

His fingers crush the rainbow into powder fine.

How many times has he crooned verse beyond the cloud

When in the sky the Goddess rides her crane divine!

He dwells here after his spirit has traveled up;

His mind is carefree as the running stream flows by.

He madly croons with sword ungirt beside wine cup;

He knows no human world but paradise on high.

Drunk, I look up and call the poet of my dreams;

My mind is pure and I see no stain in four seas.

Where is your soul in the mountain steeped in moonbeams?

Where can I find your face but in the vernal breeze?

---

① Where the immortal poet Li Bai (701–762) lived and wrote poems on
peach blossoms and on an immortal riding the crane.

ON PARTING GRIEF

How bitter parting grief is! lo!

How lush on Southern Plain the vernal grasses grow!

How endless streams before the royal temple flow!

The queens' green robes at sunset undulate like waves;

The tall bamboos are dyed in red tears at their graves.[1]

Don't you hear Lady Yu[2] in her besieged tent weep,

Surprised at the besiegers' song when night was deep?

The beauty left the hero, shedding tears in flood;

She killed herself and let the grass reddened with blood.

What do we call the parting grief, alas!

The broken heart is heard just as a broken brass.

Why not cut down the tear-specked bamboo, though slender,

And mow the blood-stained grass,

Lest parting grief should grow and break your heart so tender?

---

[1] The sister queens wept over the death of Emperor Shun (2255–2205 BC), their tears specked the bamboo and they drowned themselves in the Dongting Lake.

[2] Lady Yu was the favorite mistress of General Xiang Yu (232–202 BC) who fought against Liu Bang for the throne, won ninety-nine battles but lost the last one, and, when besieged by Liu's army, committed suicide with Lady Yu.

Wang Mian (?–1359)

ON MUME BLOSSOMS

When the violent northern wind blows, man would fall;
There is no place on earth but overspread with sand.
The Tartars frozen to death beneath the Great Wall,
Who knows mume blossoms still bring spring to southern land?

TO MUME BLOSSOMS

In the third moon the snow melts when the east wind blows;
The lakeside southern hills seem sprinkled with green dew.
Where comes the dirge of Tartar flute nobody knows?
Your countless fallen petals blot bridges out of view.

Yang Weizhen (1296–1370)

WRITTEN AT RANDOM

My western neighbor wept o'er sudden death last night;
Dismissed today, my east neighbor grieves at his plight.
We do not know whate'er tomorrow will come by.
Why in our life do we not drink our wine cup dry?

LOVESICKNESS

The lass deep in love longs for her beloved apart;
In moonlit breezy night lovesickness gnaws her heart.
Why won't she drink like silly maiden in the east,
Who cares nor for the breeze nor the moon in the least?

WATERFALL OF MOUNT LU

Like a river of stars the waterfall runs down,

It flows before the peaks which five old men's heads crown.

A silk roll woven by the fairy queen on high,

And unrolled from the loom hangs from the azure sky.

I want to cut, a pair of scissors sharp in hand,

From the white roll a misty or crystalline band.

I see the poet of cloud over stone,[1]

Like the immortal trying to catch the moon[2].

Thirsty for wine at night, what could he do but try

To ride the whale and drink the sea till it goes dry?

The water drunk turns to endless cataract here,

Hanging like jade rainbow o'er abyss cold and clear.

---

[1] The poet of cloud over stone refers to Guan Yunshi.

[2] The immortal refers to Li Bai (701–762), who, drunk, tried to catch the reflection of the moon in the river and was drowned.

WEST LAKE'S BAMBOO BRANCH SONGS IV

Do not ascend the Southern Peak, I pray, my dear!
Be sure I on the Northern Peak will not appear.
The one is veiled in cloud and the other in shower,
When will your cloud bring shower for my thirsty flower.[1]

---

[1] The speaker is a maiden living by the side of West Lake.

Ni Zan (1306–1374)

BAMBOO BRANCH SONGS

I

The rosy-dressed girls live by lakeside as they please;
In spring they will not gather leaves of mulberries.
They learn to dance like swallows in the vernal breeze;
To wed the gallant Northerners and live at ease.①

II

The old men talk about the kingdom's fall and rise;
For captive king and general slain②they give deep sighs.
At dusk the wind breaks willow branch with might and main;
The overbrimming lake is veiled in mist and rain.

---

① A satire against the Southern girls trying to wed the rich Northern conquerors.

② General Yue Fei (1103–1141) slain by the Song emperor who would not recover the lost land lest the captive emperor's return should dethrone him.

MING DYNASTY
(1368–1644)

Zhang Yining (1301–1370)

THE FISHING SITE OF YAN GUANG[1]

Your friend riding the red dragon mounted the throne;
You were left in sheep skin to fish moonbeams alone.
Though not a lord, Confucius' fame fore'er shines bright;
The emperor of lords and ministers made light.
When you shared royal bed, stars trembled in the sky;
Now you're gone, leaving water clear and mountains high.
I would fish with long, long rod and line by the side
Of Eastern Sea and sit to watch the rising tide.

---

[1] Yan Guang was a friend of Liu Xiu (6 BC–AD 57) who became the first emperor of the Eastern Han Dynasty. Yan shared the royal bed one night and then returned to fish by the Eastern Sea, for a fisherman was better than a minister of whom the emperor made light.

Song Lian (1310–1381)

A SOUTHERN SONG

I think of and long tor my lover day and night;
We're like the two blades of a pair of scissors bright.
But now one blade is up and the other is down.
When will the blades unite to cut a wedding gown?

A MORNING TRIP

At dawn cocks crow once and again;
I drive my car along the plain.
The autumn wind's severe and drear;
The morning moon is bright and clear.
In this glassy world crystalline
Goes the lonely body of mine.
My heart and soul like snow and ice.
My hair and beard clean up and nice.
I seem to breathe primitive air;
I feel free from worry and care.
Where's the immortal to impart
What now I feel deep in my heart?

Liu Ji[1] (1311–1375)

THE SILKWORM

Why should the silkworm busy alone and forget

It will be boiled when its cocoon is made one day?

Why not imitate the spider spinning its net

To catch all insects, careless of what people say?

---

[1] The poet helped the first Ming emperor to overthrow the Yuan Dynasty and establish the Ming Dynasty. This won him an earldom, but a false charge brought about his death.

POURING RAIN ON THE 19TH DAY OF THE 5TH MOON

The driving wind and rain pour on the city high;

The thunder weighed down by heavy clouds rumbles long.

After the rain we know not where the dragons[1] fly;

A pool green with grass echoes with frogs' choral song.

---

[1] The dragons were believed in ancient China to be in charge of rain.

Yuan Kai[1]

SITTING AT NIGHT IN AN ALIEN LAND

Leaves fall shower by shower on the river long.
Where can the way to my native garden be found?
The wild geese pierce the midnight rain with their new song.
O how can my heart not break on my way homebound!

---

[1] Persecuted by the emperor, Yuan Kai escaped death only by pretending to be mad.

Yang Ji (1325–?)

IN FLAT-TOP MOUNTAIN

Drizzling rain's grizzled violet flowers on the trees;
The loquat fruit is ripened by the southern breeze.
Walking slowly, I ignore the mountain path long;
On homeward way I hear but gold orioles' song.

THE YUEYANG TOWER[①]

I drink spring at the height,
Rails mirrored in the lake.
Three States with water white;
Nine peaks blue without break.
Fishes dance with delight;
The queen's soul comes awake.
Who plays on flute at night?
Wind and rain weep for her sake.

---

① The Yueyang Tower stands by the side of Dongting Lake where the queen of Emperor Shun was drowned after the emperor's death in 2205 BC.

Zhang Yu (1333–1385)

LATE SPRING IN THE NORTH[1]

By Golden Riverside the homesick cuckoos cry;
At the Jade Fountain Hill the willow catkins fly.
Three thousand miles between the north and the south stand.
Why can't I go, when spring is gone, to my homeland?

---

[1] Banished by the emperor, Zhang Yu committed suicide on the way.
The Golden River and the Jade Fountain Hill are in modern Beijing.

Xu Ben[1] (?–1379)

TO LOTUS BLOOMS AFTER RAIN

When it turns fine after rain I pass by the pool;
The lonely lotus blooms on cold waves are annoyed.
Do not say Autumn looks indifferent and cool.
What if in vernal breeze your beauty's not enjoyed?

---

[1] Xu Ben died in prison.

Gao Qi[①] (1336–1374)

WASHING MY HANDS

I love spring water where I wash my hand;

Its fragrant hue should dye both hands in green.

Its wavelets rise and fall towards the land;

The startled fish hide themselves deep, unseen.

Melancholy, I sit down on the sand.

How can I scoop up floating petals clean?

---

① The poet wrote satirical poems, offended the emperor and was put to
death after false charges were brought against him.

TO THE MUME BLOSSOM

You should dwell in the crystalline palace on high.

Who has planted you on southern shore far and nigh?

A hermit lives in mountains covered by snow white;

A beauty comes to the grove when the moon shines bright.

The shivering bamboo lends you its shadow slender;

The outspread moss would hide your fragrant petals tender.

Once the mume-lover gone, no more poet can please.

How long have you bloomed in the lonely vernal breeze?

ON A VISIT

I cross stream after stream,
And view flowers on flowers.
I arrive as in dream,
Glad to forget the hours.

HUSKING RICE

The wife is husking rice till late into the night,
Alone in thatched cottage cold with wind and rain.
She tells her baby not to cry by candlelight,
For early risers need their meal to start again.

Xie Jin (1369–1415)

FOR MY NEPHEW[1]

I thank my nephew seeing me off on the stream;
His love is deep as the River by Rocky Height.

Six years we'er passed together as if in a dream;
It seems not so long as one cozy hour last night.

---

[1] Editor in general of Imperial Academy, the poet was banished to Guangxi in 1407 when he wrote this quatrain. He died in prison seven years later.

Fang Xiaoru[1] (1357–1402)

ON MY WAY TO THE CAPITAL

The trees shed leaves in autumn late;
The Southern Plain looks desolate.

I see in boat blue hills recede
And white birds fly away in speed.

I hear men talk in accent queer;
I drown my grief in wine more dear.

What is the use of vain renown?
Though ill, I must trudge up and down.

---

[1] Summoned to the capital to legalize the new emperor, the poet disobeyed and was put to death together with hundreds of his kinsmen.

Yu Qian[1] (1398—1457)

SONG OF THE LIME

You come out of deep mountains after hammer blows;
Under fire and water tortures you're not in woes.
Though broken into pieces, you will have no fright;
You'll purify the world by washing it e'er white.

---

[1] Minister of war, Yu Qian beat back the foe who had captured the emperor in 1449, but was put to death after the emperor's restoration.

ON A COLD NEW YEAR'S EVE

I tell those who roam
To make light of cold.
Spring wind will soon come
Eastwards as foretold[1].

---

[1] The last verse may be compared with that of Shelley's Ode to the West Wind written 400 years later.

Shen Zhou (1427–1509)

A BEAUTY PLUCKING FLOWERS[1]

Last year when he left her, flowers were in full bloom;
Now flowers bloom again, but he's still in strange land.
In red and violet flowers she sees grief and gloom.
Why should the spring wind blow their grief into her hand?

---

[1] The poet was a painter and this quatrain was written on a picture he painted.

Li Dongyang (1447–1516)

THE MOUNTAINSIDE TEMPLE

The frowning peak overlooks the southern riverside;
A serpentine footpath winds up the spiral hill.
Two pathways meet among the pines and firs green-dyed;
Amid the wind and rain a lonely mook feels chill.
Flat sand and shallow grass stretch as far as the skies;
The town across the stream at sunset can be seen.
Northern and southern countries come into my eyes;
To hear the partridges sing alone on rails I lean.

Zhu Yunming (1460–1526)

TWO ORALLY COMPOSED STANZAS

I

I've six fingers and my forehead sprinkled with grey;
Forsaken by all, still my arrogance will stay.
From now on I will make friends with those ancient sages,
Ten years of golden and ten years of silver ages.

II

Not in proper attire and with disheveled hair,
I walk in corridor to and fro, here and there.
At mid-court I lie down and look upwards carefree
As fish swimming around fairy isles in the sea.

A SPRING DAY[1]

A sprig of mume in bloom welcomes the break of day;

Spring in my thatched cottage sheds its beaming ray.

With flowers in view, wine to drink and verse to read,

What better fortune can fall to scholars indeed!

---

[1] The 21st day of the 12th moon, 1493. —Note of the poet.

Tang Yin[1] (1470–1523)

THE WESTERN GATE OF SUZHOU

The capital of Wu is earthly paradise;

As Western Gate nowhere's so prosperous and nice.

Three thousand green-sleeved beauties upstair and downstair;

A million gold coins spent east or west, here and there.

From dawn to dusk the market uproar runs e'er high;

People speak different dialects from far and nigh.

If a painter is told to draw in black and white,

Of this magnificent picture he can't make light.

---

[1] Tang Yin, son of a rich merchant of Suzhou (capital of the ancient
kingdom of Wu), won the first honor in district exam at the age of 16
and in provincial exam at 29, but failed in the court exam and came
back to live on painting.

REFLECTIONS

I seek no drink divine nor meditation deep[1];

Hungry, I take my meal, and tired, I go to sleep.

I live on selling verse and pictures as I please;

I rove among red flowers and green willow trees.

My face grows old from year to year in mirror bright;

My wife and I enjoy candlelight as moonlight.

I drink till drunk as often as I enjoy pleasure;

An immortal on earth, I love my life of leisure.

---

[1] Taoist elixir and Buddhist meditation.

SONG OF PEACH BLOSSOM COTTAGE

In the Peach Blossom Land there is a peach blossom plot;
A peach blossom lover lives in Peach Blossom Cot.
The peach blossom lover plants peach trees in days fine;
He sells his peach blossoms for money to buy wine.
When he is not drunk, he would sit before the flowers;
He would lie beneath them to spend his drunken hours.
From day to day half-drunk, half-sober he'd appear;
The peach flowers blossom and fall from year to year.
I would grow old and die among flowers and wine,
Rather than bow before the steed and carriage fine.
The rich may love their dust-raising carriages and bowers;
The poor only enjoy their cup of wine and flowers.
If you compare the poor with the rich low and high,
You'll find the one on earth, the other in the sky.
If you compare the poor with the carriage and steed,
The poor have leisure while the rich gallop with speed.
Others may pity me so foolish and so mad;
I laugh at them for those who can't see through are sad.
Can you find where the tombs of gallant heroes stand?
Without flowers or wine they turn into ploughland.

SONG OF A YEAR

There are three hundred and sixty days in a year;
Spring, summer, autumn, winter, each has ninety days.
It's hard to bear in winter biting cold severe;
In summer it is boiling hot as in a blaze.
The third and ninth moons in spring and autumn are mild;
But in mild days there's cutting wind or driving rain.
On counting up, few days are fine but many wild;
Without fine scenery, fine days are passed in vain.
If we should meet fine scenery when days are fine.
Together we'd make merry and delight our heart.
If we did not light candles bright and drink sweet wine,
We might misspend our life and play not well our part.
How wise is the motto said by the sage of old.
We should enjoy by candlelight sweet vernal flowers!
One vernal hour is worth a thousand coins of gold;
I say a thousand coins can't buy back vernal hours.

Wen Zhengming (1470–1559)

THE LAKE OF STONE

The mist on Lake of Stone blends with the waves in view;

A riot of birds' songs break blooming flowers' dream.

Fragrant grass grows on hills with tea trees drenched in dew;

A painted bridge across the Southern Beauty's Stream.

The cool breeze gently ripples duckweed far and near;

The bygones lie beyond the sunset in the west.

On autumn waves again sinks the moon as last year;

A broken heart should not sing "the Crow in the Nest."[1]

---

[1] The poet was broken-hearted because he was not at home while the crow was in its nest.

Li Mengyang (1472–1529)

AUTUMN ON THE FRONTIER

The Yellow River girds the Great Wall on frontier;
Rows of wild geese in autumn breeze honk sad and drear.
The soldiers cross the trench to pursue the wild horse;
The general shoots his arrows on the Tartar force[1].
At ancient ferries dust darkens the food supply;
The battlefield is chilled by pale moon in pale sky.
It is said in the north that many heroes stand.
But who will now, like General Guo, defend the land?

---

[1] General Guo defeated the rebels who revolted against the Tang emperor in 755.

Wang Shouren (1472–1529)

ON A STORMY SEA[1]

The weal and woe which stay not in mind will pass by
Just as the floating cloud sailing across the sky.
I cross billows for miles and miles at dead of night
Like an immortal, cane in hand, riding moonlight.

---

[1] The poet was a philosopher extolling the power of mind over matter, so he could remain calm on a perilous sea.

Wang Tingxiang (1474–1544)

ANCIENT TOMBS

Old tombs lie under withered grass;
Over it cries the crow, alas!
The dead within hear not its cry;
Alone is grieved the passer-by.

Bian Gong (1476–1532)

FOR A HOME-GOING FRIEND

The moon o'er River Han shines on home-coming one,
Who goes for miles in autumn breeze like wafting leaf.
Wash not your journey dress when your journey is done!
It bears the capital's dust and our parting grief.

Xu Zhenqing (1479–1511)

A ROADSIDE VIEW

On winding hillside road peach blossoms come in sight,
But I must hurry, for the sun sheds slanting ray.
How could I with my whip of jade retain daylight!
With vernal grief at heart I must go on my way.

He Jingming (1483–1524)

SONG OF THE AUTUMN RIVER

Gray mists hower,

Waves flow away.

White dew spreads over

Grasses which sway.

Like ripples beam

Reeds on the sands.

The wind blows off my old

Hat, my short hair feels cold.

Afloat mid-stream

A beauty stands.

Her boat with mast and sail is steeped in evening rain;

At sunset in her curtained bower we remain.

While in her boat, she gathers lotus blossoms red;

Before her bower grass feels sad on which we tread.

Sweet grass in glooms

For west wind's high;

Red lotus blooms

On green waves lie.

Drunk, I sail down for miles on the river silk-white;

The moon seems steeped in water, the stream in moonlight.

Yang Shen①(1488–1559)

THE WILLOW

The weeping willow tree o'er fragrant spring holds sway;

Its yellow sprout looks like gold claw on Cold Food Day. ②

Flower-like willow down enchants the boundless sky;

It flies like snow or moth of jade in warm wind high.

It weeps on seeing people part on river wide;

Its broken twigs are cast by the bridge or roadside.

My heart breaks 'neath the moon on willowless frontier;

Severed by willow screen, my love sheds tear on tear.

---

① The poet won the first honor in imperial exam of 1511, and was banished to Yunnan for over thirty years.

② On Cold Food Day Chinese people used to take cold meals and visit their ancestral graveyard.

Huang E[1] (1498–1569)

TO MY HUSBAND

I'm tired of sending letters to far-off frontier;

So long have we been separated from year to year.

My beloved cannot come home with his longing eyes;

Where on green mountains do we not hear cuckoo's cries[2]!

---

[1] Huang E was the wife of Yang Shen.

[2] The cuckoo seems to cry in Chinese: "Better go home"!

Xie Zhen (1495–1575)

MISSING MY YOUNGER BROTHER ON AN AUTUMN DAY

I pity you who live on cutting grass and wood;

Starting when seasons change, I still delay my way.

Severed for years, our children have grown to manhood;

Out of sight, miles apart we pass each lonely day.

How much do falling autumn leaves sadden our ears?

Have rainy night and flickering lamp brought you dreams?

I miss our native garden where we shed hot tears;

Again I hear wild geese across cold lakes and streams.

Wu Cheng'en [1] (1506–1582)

THE AUTUMN MOON [2]

'Tis said a fair lady on high
Resides in the moon up the sky.
With whom her solitude to share?
An ugly toad and a jade hare.
On icy moon there is no clay;
The rootless laurel tree can't stay.
How can its golden grains appear
So abundant from year to year?
Shut up for long years in her place,
How is now her beautiful face?
I am so near her moon of jade
When it shines on my balustrade.
Moon, will you drink a cup of wine
To her loneliness as to mine?

---

[1] Wu Cheng'en was the author of *The Journey to the West*.

[2] It was said that a beautiful lady drank the elixir of immortality, flew to the moon and lived there lonely with a hare of jade and an ugly toad beside a laurel tree.

Li Panlong (1514—1570)

FAREWELL TO A BANISHED FRIEND

Green maple leaves are shivering in dreary rain:
Autumn is veiled in mist on far-off Southern plain.
Who would pity my banished friend in lonely boat?
Only white clouds across the endless river float.

Yang Jisheng[1] (1516—1555)

ON MOUNT TAI

The world's small east to west
When I climb mountains high.
I look up from the crest:
Higher white clouds sail by.

---

[1] Yang Jisheng was minister of war sentenced to death for he impeached the prime minister of treason.

Xu Wei (1521—1593)

THE SLEEPING BEAUTY[1]

The chaste rouge spot on her fair arm removed last night,
'Mid grass before jade steps are drunk the dragonflies.
The breeze brings out of palace walls the fragrance light;
Nobody knows it comes from where Lady Yang lies.
Her crimson robe revealed through gauze curtain unfurled,
She sleeps like rosy jade in autumn water sunk.
The painted beauty could still fascinate the world;
No wonder with live beauty the emperor's drunk.
I try to wake her up by calling birds to sing,
So I arouse the parrot in the western bower.
At sunset she would go to bathe in the warm spring,
Still dreaming of fresh shower for her thirsting flower.

---

[1] This poem was written on a picture of Lady Yang (719–756), beautiful mistress of Emperor Xuan Zong of the Tang Dynasty.

Wang Shizhen (1526–1590)

GENERAL QI'S SWORD[1]

Can thousand coins of gold buy a sword of this kind?
Each inch of steel reveals a battle-hardened mind.
For royal favor of his life he has made light:
No general but has suffered wind and rain at night.

---

[1] This sword was a gift of General Qi Jiguang for the poet. The general was out of favor with the emperor.

Li Zhi[1] (1527–1602)

SITTING ALONE

With friends I open wide my eyes;
Friendless, I speak to falling flowers.
The slender grass in warm wind sighs;
On sparkling sand cool moonlight showers.
Life seems a dream in countries strange;
Companions make me forget home.
My lute and books I won't arrange;
I sit to see evening cloud roam.

---

[1] The poet was an independent philosopher, put to death for his unconventional views.

Qi Jiguang[1] (1528–1587)

MARCH AT DAWN

Our banners undulate along the winding stream
Without disturbing the riverside birds from their dream.
Suddenly we beat drums and blow our bugles shrill
To startle even the deaf old monk beyond the hill.

---

[1] Qi Jiguang was a general who had won many victories against Japanese invaders.

Tang Xianzu[1] (1550–1616)

THE PEONY PAVILION

Autumn looks green as spring before my Hall of Jade;
The *Peony Pavilion* is sung here and there.
I find no connoisseur, tapping the balustrade;
Sandal clappers in hand, I teach my actress fair.

---

[1] Tang Xianzu was a contemporary of Shakespeare and playwright of "Four Dreams", of which the most famous was *Dream in Peony Pavilion*.

Gao Panlong (1562–1626)

PILLOWING ON A STONE

As running stream my heart is clean;
Like floating cloud my body's light.
In silence deep of mountains green;
The temple bell rings out of sight.

Yuan Hongdao (1568–1610)

EVENING VIEW

The east wind blows, at Red Tower trees burst in bloom;
Alone on hilltop at sunset I fall in gloom.
I'm grieved to see the dust under the horsehoof rise
And turn into a mist before wayfarers' eyes.
Below blue hills the sun is sinking by and by;
A frozen bird in dreary garden gives a cry.
By roadside sinks the monument of ancient day;
Before the hero's tomb e'en the stone horse would neigh.

Yuan Zhongdao (1570–1632)

FOUNTAIN IN MOONLIGHT

On whitened hills birds start their cries;
Congealed with cold, frost on rocks lies.
Steeped in moonlight, the fountains flow;
They turn into a stream of snow.

Feng Xiaoqing [1]

ON READING THE PEONY PAVILION

How can I bear to hear cold rain beat window panes?
I light my lamp to read *Pavilion of Peony*.
The beauty died of love, in dreams she still remains;
She's not so lonely, heart-broken as dreamless me.

---

[1] Feng Xiaoqing was mistress of Feng Qianqiu whose wife forbade her to leave a lonely islet in West Lake. She died at the age of 18 and was buried by the lakeside.

[2] See Tang Xianzu's *Dream in Peony Pavilion*.

Chen Zilong[1] (1608–1647)

ON THE 13TH NIGHT OF THE 7TH MOON

On the 13th night of the 7th moon in 1640,

I returned from the capital, met with Zhang and talked with him till dawn.

Tonight I moor my boat at the same place, but Zhang is dead and gone.

I moor my boat at sunset 'neath the maple trees;

Gone is the long, long night when we talked at ease.

How can I bear the moon together viewed last year?

The Southern River grows deeper with tear on tear.

---

[1] Chen Zilong was a leader of the anti-Manchurian forces, who drowned himself when defeated.

Xia Wanchun [1] (1631–1647)

ADIEU, MY HOMELAND

I struggled three long years,
Captive again today.
My land's worth bitter tears.
Could I come homeward way?
I know my death is near;
It's hard to leave my land.
See when my soul comes here,
I'll wave my flag in hand.

---

[1] The poet carried out anti-Manchurian activities at the age of fifteen and was put to death at seventeen.

Qing Dynasty
(1644–1911)

Qian Qianyi[1] (1582–1664)

VIEW FROM THE GARDEN OF DING

The willow down[2] afield waits for the evening tide[3];
A painted bridge leads to Peach Leaf[4] by riverside.
At sunset water-limpid spring attracts my gaze.
O where's the splendor of the Six Dynasties[5] days!

---

[1] Qian Qianyi was one of the first Ming scholar-officials who declared his allegiance to the Qing conquerors, and was then accused of plotting against the Qing emperor.

[2] The willow down may hint at the poet's favorite mistress Liu Rushi who living in the Garden of Ding, advised the poet to resist the Qing conquerors.

[3] The evening tide may refer to the restoration of the Ming Dynasty.

[4] The Peach Leaf was the Ferry where a Jing poet parted with his love. It alludes to the Ferry where Qian parted with Liu.

[5] The Six Dynasties (221–280, 317–589) had their capital at Nanjing. They allude to the Ming Dynasty.

THE ORCHID FLOWER[1]

Not living side by side but loving heart to heart,
This fragrant grass indeed may be called Orchid Flower.
Unlike the common lakeside grass which grows apart,
Her dewy eyes attract her love from hour to hour.

---

① The orchid flower may symbolize the poet's favorite mistress Liu Rushi.

Liu Rushi[1] (1618–1664)

WEST LAKE

The weeping willows stand east of the curtained bowers;
Orioles and butterflies pass through the faded flowers.
But peach blossoms on Cold Food Day are beautified
By beauties living or buried by the lakeside[2].

---

① The poetess was first in love with Chen Zilong who resisted the Qing
conquerors and drowned himself when defeated. At last, she was
wedded to Qian Qianyi.
② General Yue Fei was the hero and Su Xiaoxiao and Feng Xiaoqing
were beauties buried by the side of West Lake.

Jin Shengtan[1] (1608–1661)

TO MY SON BEFORE MY DEATH

Our blood relationship seems remote though it's near;
You follow my shadow only when books appear.
Today we are as far apart as it could be,
But the belief in Buddhism would make me free.

---

① The poet was put to death because he was accused of weeping in the
ancestral temple of the Ming emperors.

TO MY READERS BEFORE MY DEATH

We're far apart as sky from earth or the four nooks;
You make light of ten thousand miles to find my books.[1]
I've left my son who loves but reading 'neath the sky.
Would you please look on him with favorable eye?

---

① The poet was the critical commentator of *Heroes of the Marsh* and
Romance of Western Bower.

Wu Weiye (1609–1671)

SONG OF THE BEAUTIFUL YUANYUAN

The emperor left the human world on a gloomy day;
The General[①] to the imperial palace fought his way.
The royal armies dressed in mourning shed their tears;
The wrathful general for his lady wielded his spears.

"Not that I love my lady captured by the foe,
But that I hate to death the rebels spreading woe.
Like lightning sweeping them away at Mountain Black,
O'er father's death I'll weep and bring my lady back."

Remember their first meeting in a nobleman's bower:
She sang and danced as beautifully as a flower.
The nobleman promised to bestow the songstress fair
On General Wu, who carried her home in sedan chair.

Born near the Flower-Washing Stream, she was a maid
Named Yuanyuan, whose charm outshone silk and brocade.
She dreamed of roving in the royal garden where
She met the king surrounded by his maidens fair.
In previous life she must have been the Fairy Queen;
Before her door there stretched a sea of water green.

---

① General Wu Sangui, whose favorite lady Yuanyuan was captured by
the peasant army, led the Qing forces in recapturing her in 1644,
resulting in the downfall of the Ming Dynasty.

On water green two oars propelled a boat in flight:
A nobleman had carried her away by might.
Who knows on such occasion what her fate would be?
Her tear-soaked robe was all that one could see.

Her bitterness ascended as high as the skies,
But no one pitied her pearly teeth, her crystal eyes.
She was ravished and shut up inside all day long,
Where she was taught to sing every ravishing song.

The general came and drank his fill till sunset.
To whom could she complain and sing her deep regret?
With our young general bright no gallant could ever vie:
While plucking flowers of the turned to her his eye.

He freed the singing bird caged behind stout bars.
How many times they crossed the Stream of Silver Stars!
But military orders commanded him to fight;
He promised to be back and left her in sad plight.

How deep his love for her! How hard again to meet!
When rebels trampled the capital beneath their feet!
Alas! the lovesick mistress in the tower high
Was taken like the willow catkin in the sky.

Her inner chamber was surrounded all about;
From the carved balustrade she's compelled to come out.
Had not our general beaten the rebel force,
How could his lady fair be rescued on a horse?

The lady on a horse was summoned to appear,
Her hair like tousled cloud, unrecovered from fear.
Two giant candles lit her to the battlefield;
Her pretty face was clouded with her tears congealed.

The general's force, while beating drums, marched its way;
A thousand chariots drove southwest without delay.
In cloud-veiled valley rose a painted tower high;
The setting moon became a mirror to her eye.

To her homeland by riverside the news soon spread
Though ten times maples bitten by frost had turned red.
The master who taught her to sing felt fortunate;
The washerwomen still remembered their lucky mate.

We're swallows pecking clods of clay to build our nest:
One flying up the tree becomes a phoenix blest.
Before a cup of wine we grieve that old we've grown;
We're glad she's married General Wu who wears a crown.

Alas! the lady's compromised by far-flung fame:

Her beauty earned for her all noblemen's acclaim.
One casket of bright pearls brought ten caskets of grief:

Her slender waist now wafted for miles like a leaf.
Blame not the breeze that blows down flowers far and nigh!
For boundless spring has come from the earth and the sky.

A peerless beauty brings a country's up and down
And earns for a gallant hero his lasting renown.
How could a woman care about the state affair?
How could our general forsake his lady fair?
His family were slain and turned to dust and clay;
Her rosy dress will shine in history for aye.

Have you not seen
In Golden Palace where the lovebirds passed the night.
The lady was too lovely to be kept out of sight?
On dusty fragrant path now only cries blackbird,
No beauty's steps are heard
Where moss in vain grows green.

With palace music changed, for miles and miles grief reigns:
Still pearly teeth and green sleeves dance on Western Plains.
If for the conquered Southern Land I sing new lay,
Like River Han will grief overflow night and day.

STOPPED BY SNOW ON MY NORTHWARD WAY[1]

Hard is the way along mighty mountains and streams;

I have just mounted my horse and dismount it now.

Yellow sand rises high and fathomless snow seems.

How can this be compared with Southern shore! O how!

---

[1] The poet was forced to leave his homeland in the South for the court in the North.

Li Yu (1611–1685)

HEART-BROKEN SONG[1]

The bygones one and all like dreams have passed away;

I'd live with fishermen in thatched cot night and day.

Can I forget your tenderness like endless thread?

Could I repay you with a stream of tears I shed?

If in another life we could be man and wife,

I would live with delight my lonely day and night.

Do not tell me to marry a beauty anew!

Could I find one on earth who knows my heart like you?

---

[1] This was an elegy written to a fair actress who was married to the poet-playwright at 13 and died at 19.

Fang Yizhi[①](1611—1671)

GOING ALONE

Dispersed are my companions dear;

I go to the woods for my part.

I've changed my name thrice in a year;

Nine words out of ten gnaw my heart.

I'm used to hear the news of war;

My grief's deepened by wind and rain.

It is not hard to be no more;

But my friend's death would cause more pain.

① The poet was a loyalist to the Ming Dynasty, failed to overthrow the
Qing Dynasty with his friends and retired to a temple in the woods.

Gu Yanwu (1613—1682)

A FRONTIER SONG[①]

In the surrendered town snow melts into dust quiet;

The birds below the Northern Mountain cry for spring.

Now in third moon orioles and flowers run riot,

The killed should come south to his wife's dream on the wing.

① This song describes the Northern frontier where Southern warriors were killed;
the South may allude to the Ming Dynasty and the North to the Qing.

Song Wan (1614–1673)

A HOUND SEEN IN A BOAT

The autumn water's bright as the reed catkins white;
The hound in a boat cannot prey as eagles light.
After eating, head bent beside the mast it lies,
Like heroes growing fat the enemy defies.

Gong Dingzi (1615–1673)

PASSING BY JINLING[1] ON THE 3RD DAY OF THE 3RD MOON

Spring grief wafts on the stream with conquered kingdom's song;
No chains could bar the foe from sailing River Long.[2]
Indulged in pleasure, kings were captured in their hall;
Green hills and streams have seen dynasties rise and fall.

---

[1] Jinling (modern Nanjing) was the capital of the Six Dynasties (221–280; 317–589).

[2] The last king of Wu indulged in pleasure tried in vain to bar the enemy ships from sailing the Yangzi River and was captured in his palace hall in 280.

Gu Mei[1] (fl.1650)

ON A PICTURE OF PEACH BLOSSOMS AND WILLOW TREES

My lover says like peach blossom my face is fair;

I say my lover's dress is green like willow tree.

When could we be transformed into lovebirds in pair,

Flying 'mid willow leaves and peach blossoms carefree?

---

[1] The poetess was the mistress of Gong Dingzi.

Wu Jiaji (1618–1684)

ON MY WIFE'S BIRTHDAY

For twenty years in thatched cot we've lived poor life;

To cook my meal and ease my grief I have my wife.

She has no time to make up before mirror bright;

We've often passed hard times until our hair grows white.

Only swallows perch on our dreary seaside beam;

Our cottage trembles like a boat on rippling stream.

I cannot buy wine to celebrate her birthday;

I still come to consult with her on what she'll say.

Shi Runzhang (1618–1683)

SNOW SCENE VIEWED FROM THE PAVILION

The riverside pavilion overlooks the sand;

Green peaks are lost where thousands of snow-crowned hills stand.

I laugh to point at the treetop where hangs cloud white,

Without knowing it is only a sail in flight.

Wang Fuzhi (1619–1692)

ELEGY ON MY DECEASED WIFE

Can I forget ten years ago this frosty day;

The morning bells broke my dream, my wife passed away?

When the lotus root snaps, it can't be joined again;

The chilly wind blows dead leaves o'er her graveside lane.

Ye Xie (1627–1703)

ON MY NATIVE STREAM

My heart runs faster than the waves like grief wide-spread,
On rapid current goes my homesick boat ahead.
Surprised to hear my native dialect left and right,
I find over the mast the moon of yore shine bright.

Zhu Yizun (1629–1709)

THE GREEN PAVILION[①]

With royal hands the Green Pavilion beautified,
Imperial carriages often visited the hillside.
Don't lean on balustrade now for a northern view!
E'en trees on thirteen royal tombs have lost green hue.

---

① The Green Pavilion in the Temple of fragrant Hill was adorned with
handwritings of Ming emperors, and the tombs of thirteen Ming
emperors were situated to its north.

Qu Dajun (1630—1696)

BEFORE THE FLOWERS[1]

Before the flowers she stands, with her shadow she roves,
To blow apart her hundred-fold dress the wind loves.
Her face is bathed in tears as bright as dewdrops white.
Why should the moon shed on her dress its silver light?

---

[1] The lonely rover may symbolize the poet thinking of the Ming Dynasty overthrown by the Qing.

Wang Shizhen[1] (1634—1711)

PASSING AGAIN BY THE VIRGIN'S TEMPLE

Her eyebrows are still green and her earrings still bright,
Clouds in the lake vie in greenness with mist-veiled trees.
I moor my boat when morning moon sheds parting light;
White lotus out of Temple door blows in wild breeze.

---

[1] The poet tried to unfold his sense by describing the scene. Clouds, trees, moon, white lotus, all remind us of the purity and chastity of the virgin for whom the temple was built.

ON RIVER QINHUAI[①]

For years my broken heart yearns for a sail in vain;

My dreams still haunt the riverside bower of yore.

The days are veiled in sheet of wind and threads of rain;

Spring's gloomy scene looks like late autumn to deplore.

---

① A sail on River Qinhuai and the riverside bower symbolize the Ming Dynasty.

Pu Songling[①] (1640–1715)

REPLY TO WANG SHIZHEN[②]

The reader is amused by my stories of ghost.

Of my plain dress and greyish hair how can I boast?

If my dreams in ten years can afford you delight,

I've not belied our talk on rainy winter night.

---

① Pu Songling was the author of *Stories of Ghosts*.

② Wang Shizhen appreciated Pu's *Stories of Ghosts*.

Hong Sheng[1] (1645–1704)

HOMESICKNESS

In trader's boat night after night,
I yearn for homeland out of sight.
Awake, I hear the Northern tongue,
In dream, I hear but Southern song.

---

① Hong Sheng was a playwright, author of *Love in Long-life Hall*, telling of the love story of the Bright Emperor of the Tang and the beautiful Lady Yang.

Kong Shangren[1] (1648–1718)

THE GRAND RIVER VIEWED FROM THE NORTHERN MOUNTAIN

The lonely iron-clad town's girt by mountains high;
Viewing autumn sunset, I sit on mountain crest.
So fast the endless River's eastwards running by;
It seems the azure sky were flying to the west.

---

① Kong Shangren was a playwright, author of *Peach Blossom Painted with Blood*.

Chen Yuwang

ON READING *PEACH BLOSSOM FAN*

None sings *The Jade Tree Song,* [①] no trace of yore in view;
In Southern palace willow trees again look new.
While young, the prince[②] in gallantry was an old hand;
He loves a beautiful woman more than his land.

---

① *The Jade Tree Song* was composed by the last emperor (553–604) of the Chen and became the symbol of a conquered kingdom.

② The last prince of the Ming Dynasty was captured as the last emperor of the Chen, one of the Southern Dynasties.

Zha Shenxing (1650–1720)

ORALLY COMPOSED ON THE BLUE STREAM

Ships come afar, we see masts high;
We hear their oars when they pass by.
Upstream we fear the beaches before;
Downstream we like them to be more.

Nolan Xingde (1654–1685)

ON THE CAPITAL OF YORE①

Both mountain hue and river song are sad and drear;
Showers of leaves on Thirteen Tombs ruffle the ear.
The Northern kings sought pleasure on the Southern shore;
The bygone dynasties need no grass to deplore.

---

① Nanjing was the capital of the Six Dynasties (211–280; 317–589) and of the early Ming, whose thirteen emperors were buried in the Thirteen Tombs and whose last emperor sought pleasure on the Southern shore and was overthrown.

Zhao Zhixin (1662–1744)

LATE AUTUMN

I perch in little bower like an oldened tree;
I croon at leisure not because autumn grieves me.
Cold hills oft bear the rays of the sun on decline;
The crescent moon prefers o'er fallen leaves to shine.
Wild geese leave shadows on waves blending with the sky;
When frosty winds sweep the land, chrysanthemums sigh.
A jar of wine before short candle at midnight,
The Dipper hanging low fades and is lost to sight.

Shen Deqian (1673–1769)

PASSING BY XUZHOU

From the pools here and there flows rippling water clean;
For miles and miles extend the fields the willows screen.
The wayfarer would feel his beard and brows turn green;
Passing the town'mid songs of cicadas unseen.

Jin Nong (1687–1764)

THE WILLOW

Beyond Heart-Broken Bridge the willows green in haste;
When friends are gone away, heart-broken are the trees.
Thousands of branches wave like dancer's slender waist;
Could scissors cut more slender leaves than vernal breeze?

Li E (1692–1752)

IN LAKESIDE PAVILION①

The hills look cold when water falls,
'Tis vernal joy my heart recalls.
The balustrade's no longer red,
My love who leaned on it is dead.

---

① This quatrain was written in memory of the poet's fair mistress who died at the age of twenty-four and was buried by the lakeside.

Zheng Xie (1693–1765)

BAMBOO IN THE ROCK

Upright stands the bamboo amid green mountains steep,
Its toothlike root in broken rock is planted deep.
It's strong and firm though struck and beaten without rest,
Careless of the wind from north or south; east or west.

WRITTEN ON A PICTURE OF BAMBOO

I listen in my office to rustling bamboo;

It seems to complain of its woe as people do.

Petty official, I should try to play my part;

To ease shivering leaf as sorrow-laden heart.

---

① This quatrain was written on a picture drawn by the poet for Governor Bao.

Ni Ruixuan (1702–1732)

HEARING FROGS

Water's clear and grass green in a pool round;

Frogs croak all day long: they are safe and sound.

No body is free but frogs in the pool;

From heavy taxes and officials' rule.

Cao Xueqin[1] (1715–1763)

LIN DAIYU'S ELEGY ON FLOWERS

As flowers fall and petals fly across the sky,
Who pities the reds that fade and the scents that die?
Softly the gossamer floats over bowers green;
Gently the willow fluff wafts to embroidered screen.

I am grieved in my chamber to see spring depart.
O where can I pour out my sorrow-laden heart?
I step through my portal, holding in hand a hoe.
On fallen petals could I bear to come and go?

The willow threads and the elm leaves are fresh and gay;
They care not if peach and plum blossoms drift away.
Both the peach and the plum will bloom again next year,
But in my broidered chamber who will then appear?

By the third moon the swallows built their fragrant nest,
But apathetically on the beam they rest.
Next year though they may peck the buds and clay again,
Can their nest on the beam of my chamber remain?

O in the three hundred and sixty days each year,
The cutting wind and biting frost make flowers sear!

---

① Cao Xueqin was the greatest novelist of the Qing Dynasty and this
elegy is selected from his novel *A Dream of Red Mansions*.

How long can their fragrant blossoms last fresh and fair?
Once when they're blown away, they can be found nowhere.

It's harder to find flowers fallen than in bloom;
Before the steps their grave-digger is filled with gloom.
Alone with hoe in hand, my tears secretly shed,
On their bare branches like drops of blood turn them red.

As twilight falls, the woeful cuckoos sing no more;
I come back with my hoe and close the double door.
Abed in dimly-lit chamber when night is still,
Cold rain pelts my window and I feel my quilt chill.

I wonder why I should be thrown in such a fret:
Is it for love of spring or is it for regret?
I love spring when it comes and regret when it goes;
It comes and goes as silently as water flows.

Last night from the courtyard a plaintive dirge was heard.
Was it sung by the soul of flower or of bird?
The bird's soul or the flower's is hard to detain;
The flowers are bashful and silent birds remain.

I long on wings to fly
With flowers to the end of the earth and the sky.
At earth's uttermost bound,
Where can I find a sweet-scented burial mound?

Why don't I shroud in silken bag the petals fair
And bury them in earth with which they'll blend fore'er?
For pure they come and pure they go,
Not sinking into dirt below.
Now they are dead, I come to bury them today.
Who can divine the date when I shall pass away?
Men laugh at my folly in burying fallen flowers.
But who will bury me when come my final hours?

See spring depart and flowers wither by and by!
This is the time when beauty must grow old and die.
One day when spring is gone and beauty dead, alas!
Who will care for the fallen bloom and buried lass?

Yuan Mei (1716–1798)

ON LADY YANG[1]

Sing not of Lady Yang's regret of days gone by!
The Silver River severs on earth as on high.
In Stone Moat Village when the man parted from his wife,
More tears were shed than in the *Palace of Long Life*.

---

[1] Lady Yang (719–756) was the favorite mistress of the emperor who
regretted they were severed in the *Palace of Long Life* just as two celestial
lovers were by the Silver River (or the Milky Way), but they ignored
their pressgang forced man and wife to sever in Stone Moat Village.

ON VERSE WRITING

It's hard to make a verse which could afford delight;
I cannot feel at ease till I write and rewrite.
An old beauty should make up like a maiden fair;
She would not show herself unless she's dressed her hair.

THE CHICKENS

The chickens eat their fill;
They're boiled when fat they grow.
The feeder's wise and will;
Not let the chickens know.

ON PUSHING OPEN THE WINDOW

All night long rain fell thick;
Doors closed, I stay inside.
At dawn hills come love-sick;
Through windows opened wide.

ELEGY ON MY WISE MISTRESS[①]

I still remember her singing *"Mulberry Song"*,
And the wedding of her beauty with my renown.
In autumn we enjoyed the southern moon for long;
In winter severed by west mountains snowflakes crown.
I relished no rich soup but prepared by her hand;
Our talk from heart to heart gave nothing but delight.
How could the twenty years we passed in southern land
Last not so long as happy dreams of vernal night?

---

① The poet's wise mistress died in autumn 1773.

Ji Yun (1724–1805)

ON RIVER RICH SPRING

Along the river hill on hill enchants the eye;
I've just come out of Hangzhou when my heart is light.
The mist-veiled emerald peaks mingle with the sky;
On a mirror of glaze is floating a sail white.

Jiang Shiquan (1725–1785)

WRITTEN ON A PICTURE

I'd paint hills not on sunny but on rainy days;
A beauty would in moistened mirror fix her gaze.
No other view than a dim one would better please;
Immortals come and go on wings of cloud or breeze.

Zhao Yi (1727–1814)

ON POETRY

Li Bai and Du Fu's verse[1] is read from mouth to mouth,
But now it cannot arouse our emotion new.
Talents emerge from age to age, from north to south,
To lead in verse for hundred years each has his due.

---

[1] Li Bai (701–762) was the greatest romantic poet and Du Fu (712–770) was the greatest realistic poet of the Tang Dynasty.

Dun Min[1]

TO CAO XUEQIN[2]

A long, long winding path leads to green hill and rill;
Ivy leaves and rainbow clouds veil your cottage still.
Gone for poetic verve, in temple cell you stay;
With money earned by pictures sold, for wine you pay.
You croon like mad in northern fair over your fate;
You dream of splendor of Southern River of late.
How much regret of old and how much sorrow new!
Drunken, you look with scorn at the poor world in view.

---

[1] Dun Min was a contemporary and good friend of Cao Xueqin.

[2] Cao Xueqin (1715–1763) was the greatest novelist of the Qing Dynasty and author of *A Dream of Red Mansions*.

Yao Nai (1731–1815)

BAMBOO BRANCH SONG ON THE RIVER

When the eastern wind blows, my love's boat upstream goes;
It will come downstream homeward when the west wind blows.
If Heaven should fulfil my hearty wish sincere,
The western wind would blow homeward for all the year.

Hu Yichang (1743–1773)

THE PEAK OF JADE

Among a riot of mountains high;
The Peak of Jade stands in mid-sky.
A thousand rocks see fountains leap;
Clouds swallow pines in valleys deep.
On steep shores southern billow run;
Over the bamboos rises the sun.
Can I not raise a long, long howl;
As empty pools hear dragons growl!

Huang Jingren (1749–1783)

PARTING FROM MY OLD MOTHER

Leave my mother at the door for riverside,
I gaze at her white hair and tearful eyes now dried.
To have on snowy night a son not within call,
It is no better than to have no son at all.

Zhang Weiping (1780–1859)

THE FIRST THUNDER[1]

Mute Nature has a feeling heart,
Spring comes to see cold winter part.
All flowers are ready to burst,
But wait for thunder to roar first.

---

[1] This quatrain written in 1824 predicts the Opium War in 1840.

Lin Zexu[1] (1785–1850)

THE WESTERNMOST STRONGHOLD

The hundred-foot-high Great Wall bars the western sky;
Having journeyed for miles and miles, I stop my steed.
The endless battlements join proud trees far and nigh;
The surrounding walls weigh on clouds flying with speed.
Steep Heaven's Mountain stands level with the stronghold;
The boundless desert come in view puzzles my eyes.
Who says the Eastern Pass is strongest as of old?
Looking back, I find only a mole-hill rise.

---

[1] Lin Zexu was a national hero who burned up the opium imported from
England in 1840, but was banished to the westernmost stronghold.

Gong Zizhen[1](1792–1841)

MISCELLANIES OF THE YEAR 1839 (V)

My parting grief is boundless when the sun sinks low;
Eastward I point my whip and far away I'll go.[1]
The fallen blossoms are not an unfeeling thing;
Though turned to mud, they'd nurture flowers' growth next spring.

---

① The poet left the court when his proffered service to Commissioner Lin Zexu was rejected.

MISCELLANIES OF THE YEAR 1839 (CXXV)

From wind and thunder comes a nation's vital force,
What a great pity not to hear a neighing horse!
I urge the Lord of Heaven[1] to brace up again,
And send down talents of all kinds to Central Plain.[2]

---

① This stanza was a prayer written for a Taoist temples; by the Lord of Heaven the poet alluded to the emperor.
② Another version of the last couplet reads as follows: O Lord of Heaven, please brace up as I beseech And send down talents to earth with freedom of speech.

Zheng Zhen (1806–1864)

ON JOURNEY IN YUNNAN

It is as hard on journey as in office room;
What I see fills my heart with wonder as with gloom.
I rest beneath first tree or in first house in view;[①]
I sleep in cowshed old or rise in pigsty new.
The fleas of yesternight meet with those of today;
The flies up and down greet each other on the way.
The exiled poet[②] might praise the eastern seaside.
What would he say in this place desolate and wide?

---

① There were few trees and few houses on the way so that the poet had to take a rest in the shade of the first tree or in the first house he saw.

② The poet refers to Su Shi (1037–1101) who was banished to the seaside but wrote poems in praise of the place.

Huang Zunxian (1848–1905)

MOUNT FUJI IN JAPAN[①]

The earth bursts forth to scrape the sky; lofty appears;

The Lotus Peak upsurging from the Eastern Sea.

The snow has lasted o'er two thousand five hundred years;

Its boundless white has purified a myriad li.

---

① Mount Fujiyama, the highest mountain in Japan, was also called Lotus Peak in Chinese, for it looked like a white lotus bloom.

Tan Sitong (1865–1898)

AT DAWN ATOP THE HIGHEST PEAK OF THE SOUTHERN MOUNTAIN[①]

Atop the peak I feel not high;

Looking around, I find no crest.

I only see clouds floating by

Now and then purify my breast.

Beyond dark earth stars sink awake;

The sun leaps up like molten gold.

From half the spoon of Dongting Lake

Dragon would rise in autumn cold.[②]

---

① The poet was a reformist put to death at the age of 33. A native of Hunan, he ascended in 1891 the highest peak of the Southern Mountain in his homeland.

② Strange to say, the "dragon" seemed to predict the rise of Mao Zedong, born in Hunan in 1893, whose verse reads: "Alone I stand in autumn cold..."

Qiu Jin[1] (1875–1907)

SONG OF THE AUTUMN WIND

All grasses yellow at the autumn breeze's song;

The autumn wind by nature's vigorous and strong.

It makes all flowers drop their head with sere leaves lost;

Alone chrysanthemums can stand against the frost.

Flowers in full bloom, they belong to yellow race;

Petal on petal, they transform the country's face.

The mirror-like full moon brightens the river clear[2].

How can't the river, wave on wave, shiver with fear?

Last night was full of autumn wind and autumn rain;

And autumn frost and autumn dew seem to complain.

The leaves no longer green fear to fall in the breeze;

The immigrating birds bewail atop the trees.

When autumn comes, the weather is so sad and drear,

And autumn thoughts prevail on old Cathay's frontier.

Beyond the border horses are ready to fight;

The angry general puts on golden armor bright.

In golden armor he fights against Hunnish foe;

Millions of Hunnish soldiers, beaten, backward go.

The general laughs and his soldiers rise at his call

To drink to Freedom at the Hunnish capital.

---

① Qiu Jin was a revolutionary martyr put to death by the Qing government.

② "Bright" is the epithet for the Ming Dynasty (1368–1644) and "clear" is that for the Qing Dynasty (1644–1911).

许译中国经典诗文集

宋元明清诗选

许渊冲　许明　译

五洲传播出版社　中华书局

宋代

陈抟

归隐

十年踪迹走红尘，回首青山入梦频。

紫陌纵荣争及睡，朱门虽贵不如贫。

愁闻剑戟扶危主，闷见笙歌聒醉人。

携取琴书归旧隐，野花啼鸟一般春。

柳开

塞上

鸣骹直上一千尺，天静无风声更干。

碧眼胡儿三百骑，尽提金勒向云看。

王禹偁

村行

马穿山径菊初黄，信马悠悠野兴长。

万壑有声含晚籁，数峰无语立斜阳。

棠梨叶落胭脂色，荞麦花开白雪香。

何事吟余忽惆怅？村桥原树似吾乡。

清明

无花无酒过清明，兴味萧然似野僧。
昨日邻家乞新火，晓窗分与读书灯。

杨朴

七夕

未会牵牛意若何？须邀织女弄金梭。
年年乞与人间巧，不道人间巧已多。

寇准

书河上亭壁

岸阔樯稀波渺茫，独凭危槛思何长。
萧萧远树疏林外，一半秋山带夕阳。

林逋

山园小梅

众芳摇落独暄妍，占尽风情向小园。
疏影横斜水清浅，暗香浮动月黄昏。
霜禽欲下先偷眼，粉蝶如知合断魂。
幸有微吟可相狎，不须檀板共金樽。

范仲淹

江上渔者

江上往来人，但爱鲈鱼美。
君看一叶舟，出没风波里。

晏殊

无题

油壁香车不再逢，峡云无迹任西东。
梨花院落溶溶月，柳絮池塘淡淡风。
几日寂寥伤酒后，一番萧索禁烟中。
鱼书欲寄何由达？水远山长处处同。

落花

坠素翻红各自伤，青楼烟雨忍相忘。

将飞更作回风舞，已落犹成半面妆。

沧海客归珠迸泪，章台人去骨遗香。

可能无意传双蝶，尽付芳心与蜜房。

鲁山山行

适与野情惬，千山高复低。

好峰随处改，幽径独行迷。

霜落熊升树，林空鹿饮溪。

人家在何许？云外一声鸡。

戏答元珍

春风疑不到天涯，二月山城未见花。

残雪压枝犹有橘，冻雷惊笋欲抽芽。

夜闻归雁生乡思，病入新年感物华。

曾是洛阳花下客，野芳虽晚不须嗟。

丰乐亭游春

红树青山日欲斜，长郊草色绿无涯。
游人不管春将老，来往亭前踏落花。

梦中作

夜凉吹笛千山月，路暗迷人百种花。
棋罢不知人换世，酒阑无奈客思家。

苏舜钦

过苏州

东出盘门刮眼明，萧萧疏雨更阴晴。
绿杨白鹭俱自得，近水远山皆有情。
万物盛衰天意在，一身羁苦俗人轻。
无穷好景无缘住，旅棹区区暮亦行。

乡思

人言落日是天涯，望极天涯不见家。
已恨碧山相阻隔，碧山还被暮云遮。

插花吟

头上花枝照酒卮，酒卮中有好花枝。
身经两世太平日，眼见四朝全盛时。
况复筋骸粗康健，那堪时节正芳菲？
酒涵花影红光溜，争忍花前不醉归？

新晴山月

高松漏疏月，落影如画地。
徘徊爱其下，夜久不能寐。
怯风池荷卷，病雨山果坠。
谁伴予苦吟？满林啼络纬。

曾巩

西楼

海浪如云去却回，北风吹起数声雷。
朱楼四面钩疏箔，卧看千山急雨来。

司马光

客中初夏

四月清和雨乍晴，南山当户转分明。
更无柳絮因风起，惟有葵花向日倾。

王安石

登飞来峰

飞来山上千寻塔，闻说鸡鸣见日升。
不畏浮云遮望眼，自缘身在最高层。

夜直

金炉香烬漏声残，剪剪轻风阵阵寒。
春色恼人眠不得，月移花影上栏杆。

泊船瓜洲

京口瓜洲一水间，钟山只隔数重山。
春风又绿江南岸，明月何时照我还？

明妃曲

明妃初出汉宫时，泪湿春风鬓脚垂。
低徊顾影无颜色，尚得君王不自持。
归来却怪丹青手，入眼平生几曾有。
意态由来画不成，当时枉杀毛延寿。
一去心知更不归，可怜着尽汉宫衣。
寄声欲问塞南事，只有年年鸿雁飞。
家人万里传消息，好在毡城莫相忆。
君不见咫尺长门闭阿娇？人生失意无南北。

元日

爆竹声中一岁除，春风送暖入屠苏。
千门万户曈曈日，总把新桃换旧符。

北陂杏花

一陂春水绕花身，花影妖娆各占春。
纵被春风吹作雪，绝胜南陌碾成尘。

书湖阴先生壁

茅檐长扫净无苔，花木成畦手自栽。
一水护田将绿绕，两山排闼送青来。

北山

北山输绿涨横陂，直堑回塘滟滟时。
细数落花因坐久，缓寻芳草得归迟。

郑獬

春尽

春尽行人未到家，春风应怪在天涯。
夜来过岭忽闻雨，今日满溪俱是花。
前树未回疑路断，后山才转便云遮。
野间绝少尘埃污，惟有清泉漾白沙。

刘攽

新晴

青苔满地初晴后，绿树无人昼梦余。
惟有南风旧相识，偷开门户又翻书。

王安国

题滕王阁

滕王平昔好追游，高阁依然枕碧流。
胜地几经兴废事，夕阳偏照古今愁。
城中树密千家市，天际人归一叶舟。
极目沧波吟不尽，西山重叠乱云浮。

王令

暑旱苦热

清风无力屠得热，落日着翅飞上山。
人固已惧江海竭，天岂不惜河汉干？
昆仑之高有积雪，蓬莱之远常遗寒。
不能手提天下往，何忍身去游其间。

春晚

三月残花落更开，小檐日日燕飞来。
子规夜半犹啼血，不信东风唤不回。

程颢

春日偶成

云淡风轻近午天，傍花随柳过前川。
时人不识余心乐，将谓偷闲学少年。

秋日偶成

闲来无事不从容，睡觉东窗日已红。
万物静观皆自得，四时佳兴与人同。
道通天地有形外，思入风云变态中。
富贵不淫贫贱乐，男儿到此是豪雄。

郊行即事

芳原绿野恣行时，春入遥山碧四围。
兴逐乱红穿柳巷，困临流水坐苔矶。
莫辞盏酒十分醉，只恐风花一片飞。
况是清明好天气，不妨游衍莫忘归。

蔡确

夏日登车盖亭

纸屏石枕竹方床，手倦抛书午梦长。
睡觉莞然成独笑，数声渔笛在沧浪。

苏轼

辛丑十一月十九日，既与子由别于郑州西门之外，马上赋诗一篇寄之

不饮胡为醉兀兀？此心已逐归鞍发。

归人犹自念庭帏，今我何以慰寂寞？

登高回首坡垅隔，但见乌帽出复没。

苦寒念尔衣裘薄，独骑瘦马踏残月。

路人行歌居人乐，童仆怪我苦凄恻。

亦知人生要有别，但恐岁月去飘忽。

寒灯相对记畴昔，夜雨何时听萧瑟？

君知此意不可忘，慎勿苦爱高官职。

腊日游孤山访惠勤惠思二僧

天欲雪，云满湖，楼台明灭山有无。

水清出石鱼可数，林深无人鸟相呼。

腊日不归对妻孥，名寻道人实自娱。

道人之居在何许？宝云山前路盘纡。

孤山孤绝谁肯庐，道人有道山不孤。

纸窗竹屋深自暖，拥褐坐睡依团蒲。

天寒路远愁仆夫，整驾催归及未晡。

出山回望云木合，但见野鹘盘浮图。

兹游淡薄欢有余，到家恍如梦蘧蘧。

作诗火急追亡逋，清景一失后难摹。

六月二十七日望湖楼醉书

黑云翻墨未遮山，白雨跳珠乱入船。
卷地风来忽吹散，望湖楼下水如天。

新城道中

东风知我欲山行，吹断檐间积雨声。
岭上晴云披絮帽，树头初日挂铜钲。
野桃含笑竹篱短，溪柳自摇沙水清。
西崦人家应最乐，煮芹烧笋饷春耕。

饮湖上初晴后雨

水光潋滟晴方好，山色空濛雨亦奇。
欲把西湖比西子，淡妆浓抹总相宜。

李思训画长江绝岛图

山苍苍，水茫茫，大孤小孤江中央。
崖崩路绝猿鸟去，惟有乔木搀天长。
客舟何处来？棹歌中流声抑扬。
沙平风软望不到，孤山久与船低昂。
峨峨两烟鬟，晓镜开新妆。
舟中贾客莫漫狂，小姑前年嫁彭郎。

百步洪

长洪斗落生跳波，轻舟南下如投梭。
水师绝叫凫雁起，乱石一线争磋磨。
有如兔走鹰隼落，骏马下注千丈坡。
断弦离柱箭脱手，飞电过隙珠翻荷。
四山眩转风掠耳，但见流沫生千涡。
险中得乐虽一快，何异水伯夸秋河。
我生乘化日夜逝，坐觉一念逾新罗。
纷纷争夺醉梦里，岂信荆棘埋铜驼？
觉来俯仰失千劫，回视此水殊委蛇。
君看岸边苍石上，古来篙眼如蜂窠。
但应此心无所住，造物虽驶如吾何！
回船上马各归去，多言哓哓师所呵。

海棠

东风袅袅泛崇光，香雾空蒙月转廊。
只恐夜深花睡去，故烧高烛照红妆。

题西林壁

横看成岭侧成峰，远近高低各不同。
不识庐山真面目，只缘身在此山中。

惠崇春江晓景

竹外桃花三两枝，春江水暖鸭先知。
蒌蒿满地芦芽短，正是河豚欲上时。

赠刘景文

荷尽已无擎雨盖，菊残犹有傲霜枝。
一年好景君须记，最是橙黄橘绿时。

纵笔

一

白头萧散满霜风，小阁藤床寄病容。
报道先生春睡美，道人轻打五更钟。

二

寂寂东坡一病翁，白须萧散满霜风。
小儿误喜朱颜在，一笑那知是酒红。

黄庭坚

夜发分宁寄杜涧叟

阳关一曲水东流，灯火旌阳一钓舟。
我自只如常日醉，满川风月替人愁。

寄黄几复

我居北海君南海，寄雁传书谢不能。
桃李春风一杯酒，江湖夜雨十年灯。
持家但有四立壁，治病不蕲三折肱。
想见读书头已白，隔溪猿哭瘴溪藤。

雨中登岳阳楼望君山二首

一

投荒万死鬓毛斑，生出瞿塘滟滪关。
未到江南先一笑，岳阳楼上对君山。

二

满川风雨独凭栏，绾结湘娥十二鬟。
可惜不当湖水面，银山堆里看青山。

鄂州南楼书事

四顾山光接水光，凭栏十里芰荷香。
清风明月无人管，并作南楼一味凉。

奉答李和甫代简二绝句

一

山色江声相与清，卷帘待得月华生。
可怜一曲并船笛，说尽故人离别情。

二

梦中往事随心见，醉里繁华乱眼生。
长为风流恼人病，不如天性总无情。

题阳关图

一

断肠声里无形影，画出无声亦断肠。
想得阳关更西路，北风低草见牛羊。

二

人事好乖当语离，龙眠貌出断肠诗。
渭城柳色关何事？自是离人作许悲。

秦观

泗州东城晚望

渺渺孤城白水环，舳舻人语夕霏间。
林梢一抹青如画，应是淮流转处山。

陈师道

十七日观潮

漫漫平沙走白虹，瑶台失手玉杯空。
晴天摇动清江底，晚日浮沉急浪中。

张耒

夏日

长夏江村风日清，檐牙燕雀已生成。
蝶衣晒粉花枝舞，蛛网添丝屋角晴。
落落疏帘邀月影，嘈嘈虚枕纳溪声。
久斑两鬓如霜雪，直欲樵渔过此生。

初见嵩山

年来鞍马困尘埃，赖有青山豁我怀。
日暮北风吹雨去，数峰清瘦出云来。

晁说之

题明王打球图

阊阖千门万户开，三郎沉醉打球回。
九龄已去韩休死，无复明朝谏疏来。

牧童
___

答钟弱翁

草铺横野六七里，笛弄晚风三四声。
归来饱饭黄昏后，不脱蓑衣卧月明。

僧惠洪
___

秋千

画架双裁翠络偏，佳人春戏小楼前。
飘扬血色裙拖地，断送玉容人上天。
花板润沾红杏雨，彩绳斜挂绿杨烟。
下来闲处从容立，疑是蟾宫谪降仙。

徐俯
___

春游湖

双飞燕子几时回？夹岸桃花蘸水开。
春雨断桥人不渡，小舟撑出柳阴来。

李纲
___

病牛

耕犁千亩实千箱，力尽筋疲谁复伤？
但得众生皆得饱，不辞羸病卧残阳。

李清照

绝句

生当作人杰，死亦为鬼雄。
至今思项羽，不肯过江东。

曾几

三衢道中

梅子黄时日日晴，小溪泛尽却山行。
绿阴不减来时路，添得黄鹂四五声。

陈与义

春寒

二月巴陵日日风，春寒未了怯园公。
海棠不惜胭脂色，独立蒙蒙细雨中。

朱淑真

清昼

竹摇清影罩幽窗，两两时禽噪夕阳。
谢却海棠飞尽絮，困人天气日初长。

惜春

连理枝头花正开，妒花风雨苦相催。
愿教青帝长为主，莫遣纷纷点翠苔。

陆游

书愤

早岁那知世事艰？中原北望气如山。
楼船夜雪瓜洲渡，铁马秋风大散关。
塞上长城空自许，镜中衰鬓已先斑。
《出师》一表真名世，千载谁堪伯仲间？

临安春雨初霁

世味年来薄似纱，谁令骑马客京华？
小楼一夜听春雨，深巷明朝卖杏花。
矮纸斜行闲作草，晴窗细乳戏分茶。
素衣莫起风尘叹，犹及清明可到家。

秋夜将晓出篱门迎凉有感

三万里河东入海，五千仞岳上摩天。
遗民泪尽胡尘里，南望王师又一年！

十一月四日风雨大作

僵卧孤村不自哀，尚思为国戍轮台。
夜阑卧听风吹雨，铁马冰河入梦来。

沈园

一

城上斜阳画角哀，沈园非复旧池台。
伤心桥下春波绿，曾是惊鸿照影来。

二

梦断香销四十年，沈园柳老不吹绵。
此身行作稽山土，犹吊遗踪一泫然！

梅花绝句

闻道梅花坼晓风，雪堆遍满四山中。
何方可化身千亿？一树梅前一放翁。

示儿

死去元知万事空，但悲不见九州同。
王师北定中原日，家祭无忘告乃翁。

范成大

横塘

南浦春来绿一川，石桥朱塔两依然。
年年送客横塘路，细雨垂杨系画船。

四时田园杂兴

一

土膏欲动雨频催，万草千花一饷开。
舍后荒畦犹绿秀，邻家鞭笋过墙来。

二

昼出耘田夜绩麻，村庄儿女各当家。
童孙未解供耕织，也傍桑阴学种瓜。

三

新筑场泥镜面平，家家打稻趁霜晴。
笑歌声里轻雷动，一夜连枷响到明。

尤袤

题米元晖潇湘图

一

万里江天杳霭，一村烟树微茫。
只欠孤篷听雨，恍如身在潇湘。

二

淡淡晓山横雾，茫茫远水平沙。
安得绿蓑青笠，往来泛宅浮家。

杨万里

伤春

准拟今春乐事浓，依然枉却一东风。
年年不带看花眼，不是愁中即病中。

闲居初夏午睡起

梅子留酸软齿牙，芭蕉分绿与窗纱。
日长睡起无情思，闲看儿童捉柳花。

晓出净慈寺送林子方

毕竟西湖六月中，风光不与四时同。
接天莲叶无穷碧，映日荷花别样红。

过松源晨炊漆公店

莫言下岭便无难，赚得行人错喜欢。
正入万山圈子里，一山放出一山拦。

林升

题临安邸

山外青山楼外楼，西湖歌舞几时休？
暖风熏得游人醉，直把杭州作汴州。

朱熹

春日

胜日寻芳泗水滨，无边光景一时新。
等闲识得东风面，万紫千红总是春。

观书有感

半亩方塘一鉴开，天光云影共徘徊。
问渠那得清如许？为有源头活水来。

泛舟

昨夜江边春水生，蒙冲巨舰一毛轻。
向来枉费推移力，此日中流自在行。

题榴花

五月榴花照眼明，枝间时见子初成。
可怜此地无车马，颠倒苍苔落绛英。

僧志南

绝句

古木阴中系短篷，杖藜扶我过桥东。
沾衣欲湿杏花雨，吹面不寒杨柳风。

张栻

立春日禊亭偶成

律回岁晚冰霜少，春到人间草木知。
便觉眼前生意满，东风吹水绿参差。

翁卷

村居即事

绿遍山原白满川，子规声里雨如烟。
乡村四月闲人少，才了蚕桑又插田。

赵师秀

约客

黄梅时节家家雨，青草池塘处处蛙。
有约不来过夜半，闲敲棋子落灯花。

戴复古

初夏游张园

乳鸭池塘水浅深，熟梅天气半晴阴。
东园载酒西园醉，摘尽枇杷一树金。

高翥

清明日对酒

南北山头多墓田，清明祭扫各纷然。
纸灰飞作白蝴蝶，泪血染成红杜鹃。
日落狐狸眠冢上，夜归儿女笑灯前。
人生有酒须当醉，一滴何曾到九泉！

刘克庄

莺梭

掷柳迁乔太有情，交交时作弄机声。
洛阳三月花如锦，多少工夫织得成？

叶绍翁

游园不值

应怜屐齿印苍苔，小叩柴扉久不开。
春色满园关不住，一枝红杏出墙来。

郑会

题邸间壁

酴醾香梦怯春寒，翠掩重门燕子闲。
敲断玉钗红烛冷，计程应说到常山。

白玉蟾

早春

南枝才放两三花，雪里吹香弄粉些。
淡淡着烟浓着月，深深笼水浅笼沙。

王淇

暮春游小园

一丛梅粉褪残妆，涂抹新红上海棠？
开到荼蘼花事了，丝丝天棘出莓墙。

梅

不受尘埃半点侵，竹篱茅舍自甘心。
只因误适林和靖，惹得诗人说到今。

雷震

村晚

草满池塘水满陂，山衔落日浸寒漪。
牧童归去横牛背，短笛无腔信口吹。

卢梅坡

雪梅

梅雪争春未肯降，骚人阁笔费评章。
梅须逊雪三分白，雪却输梅一段香。

文天祥

过零丁洋

辛苦遭逢起一经，干戈寥落四周星。
山河破碎风飘絮，身世浮沉雨打萍。
惶恐滩头说惶恐，零丁洋里叹零丁。
人生自古谁无死？留取丹心照汗青。

金陵驿

草合离宫转夕晖，孤云飘泊复何依？
山河风景元无异，城郭人民半已非。
满地芦花和我老，旧家燕子傍谁飞？
从今别却江南路，化作啼鹃带血归。

元代

郝经

落花

彩云红雨暗长门，翡翠枝余萼绿痕。
桃李东风蝴蝶梦，关山明月杜鹃魂。
玉阑烟冷空千树，金谷香销谩一尊。
狼藉满庭君莫扫，且留春色到黄昏。

陈孚

博浪沙

一击车中胆气豪，祖龙社稷已惊摇。
如何十二金人外，犹有民间铁未销？

江天暮雪

长空卷玉花，汀洲白浩浩。
雁影不复见，千崖暮如晓。
渔翁寒欲归，不记巴陵道。
坐睡船自流，云深一蓑小。

金山寺

万顷天光俯可吞，壶中别有小乾坤。
云侵塔影横江口，潮送钟声过海门。
僧榻夜随鲛室涌，佛灯秋隔蜃楼昏。
年年只有中泠水，不受人间一点尘。

居庸叠翠

断崖万仞如削铁，鸟飞不度苔石裂。
嵯岈老树无碧柯，六月太阴飞急雪。
寒沙茫茫出关道，骆驼夜吼黄云老。
征鸿一声起长空，风吹草低山月小。

戴表元

感旧歌者

牡丹红紫艳春天，檀板朱丝锦色笺。
头白江南一尊酒，无人知是李龟年。

白雁行

北风初起易水寒，北风再起吹江干。

北风三吹白雁来，寒气直薄朱崖山。

乾坤噫气三百年，一风扫地无留残。

万里江湖想潇洒，伫看春水雁来还。

山家

马蹄踏水乱明霞，醉袖迎风受落花。

怪见溪童出门望，鹊声先我到山家。

观梅有感

东风吹落战尘沙，梦想西湖处士家。

只恐江南春意减，此心元不为梅花。

山中月夕

满怀幽思自萧萧，况对空山夜正遥。

四壁晴秋霜着色，一天明水月生潮。

歌传岩谷声豪宕，酒泛星河影动摇。

醉里似闻猿鹤语，百年人境有今朝。

赵孟頫

岳鄂王墓

鄂王墓上草离离，秋日荒凉石兽危。
南渡君臣轻社稷，中原父老望旌旗。
英雄已死嗟何及，天下中分遂不支。
莫向西湖歌此曲，水光山色不胜悲。

绝句

春寒恻恻掩重门，金鸭香残火尚温。
燕子不来花又落，一庭风雨自黄昏。

纪旧游

二月江南莺乱飞，百花开谢柳依依。
落红无数迷歌扇，嫩绿多情妒舞衣。
金鸭焚香川上暝，画船挝鼓月中归。
如今寂寞东风里，把酒无言对夕晖。

绝句

溪头月色白如沙，近水楼台一万家。
谁向夜深吹玉笛？伤心莫听后庭花。

杨载

宗阳宫望月

老君堂上凉如水，坐看冰轮转二更。

大地山河微有影，九天风露寂无声。

蛟龙并起承金榜，鸾凤双飞载玉笙。

不信弱流三万里，此身今夕到蓬瀛。

宿浚仪公湖亭

两两三三白鸟飞，背人斜去落渔矶。

雨余不遣浓云散，犹向山前拥翠微。

到京师

城雪初消荠菜生，角门深巷少人行。

柳梢听得黄鹂语，此是春来第一声。

暮春游西湖北山

愁耳偏工着雨声，好怀常恐负山行。

未辞花事骎骎盛，正喜湖光淡淡晴。

倦憩客犹勤访寺，幽栖吾欲厌归城。

绿畴桑麦盘樱笋，因忆离家恰岁更。

范梈

离扬州

孤篷如磨绕汀沙，叶满平湖藕未花。
回首竹西亭渐远，一江烟雨酒旗斜。

掘冢歌

昨日旧冢掘，今朝新冢成。
冢前两翁仲，送旧还迎新。
旧魂未出新魂入，旧魂还对新魂泣。
旧魂丁宁语新魂，好地不用多子孙。
子孙绵绵如不绝，曾孙不掘玄孙掘。
我今掘矣良可悲，不知君掘又何时。

虞集

白翎雀歌

乌桓城下白翎雀，雌雄相呼以为乐。
平沙无树托营巢，八月雪深黄草薄。
君不见旧时飞燕在昭阳，沉沉宫殿锁鸳鸯。
芙蓉露冷秋宵永，芍药风暄春昼长。

院中独坐

何处它年寄此生，山中江上总关情。
无端绕屋长松树，尽把风声作雨声。

挽文丞相

徒把金戈挽落晖，南冠无奈北风吹。
子房本为韩仇出，诸葛宁知汉祚移？
云暗鼎湖龙去远，月明华表鹤归迟。
不须更上新亭望，大不如前洒泪时。

至正改元辛巳寒食日示弟及诸子侄

江山信美非吾土，飘泊栖迟近百年。
山舍墓田同水曲，不堪梦觉听啼鹃。

送袁伯长扈从上京

日色苍茫映赭袍，时巡毋乃圣躬劳。
天连阁道晨留辇，星散周庐夜属橐。
白马锦鞯来窈窕，紫驼银瓮出葡萄。
从官车骑多如雨，只有扬雄赋最高。

萨都剌

燕姬曲

燕京女儿十六七，颜如花红眼如漆。
兰香满路马尘飞，翠袖短鞭娇欲滴。
春风澹荡摇春心，银筝华烛高堂深。
绣衾不暖锦鸳梦，紫帘垂雾天沉沉。
芳年谁惜去如水？春困着人倦梳洗。
夜来小雨润天街，满院杨花飞不起。

芙蓉曲

秋江渺渺芙蓉芳，秋江女儿将断肠。
绛袍春浅护云暖，翠袖日暮迎风凉。
鲤鱼吹浪江波白，霜落洞庭飞木叶。
荡舟何处采莲人，爱惜芙蓉好颜色。

上京即事二首

一

牛羊散漫落日下，野草生香乳酪甜。
卷地朔风沙似雪，家家行帐下毡帘。

二

紫塞风高弓力强，王孙走马猎沙场。
呼鹰腰箭归来晚，马上倒悬双白狼。

石夫人

危危独立向江滨，四伴无人水作邻。
绿鬓懒梳千载髻，朱颜不改万年春。
雪为腻粉凭风傅，露作胭脂仗日匀。
莫道脸前无宝镜，一轮明月照夫人。

揭傒斯

夏五月武昌舟中触目

两髯背立鸣双橹，短蓑开合沧江雨。
青山如龙入云去，白发何人并沙语？
船头放歌船尾和，篷上雨鸣篷下坐。
推篷不省是何乡，但见双双白鸥过。

和欧阳南阳月夜思

一

月出照中园，邻家犹未眠。
不嫌风露冷，看到树阴圆。

二

天清照逾近，夜久月将远。
墙东双白杨，秋声隔窗满。

别武昌

欲归常恨迟，将行反愁遽。
残年念骨肉，久客多亲故。
伫立望江波，江波正东注。

寒夜作

疏星冻霜空，流月湿林薄。
虚馆人不眠，时闻一叶落。

归舟

汀洲春草遍，风雨独归时。
大舸中流下，青山两岸移。
鸦啼木郎庙，人祭水神祠。
波浪争掀舞，艰难久自知。

张雨

湖州竹枝词

临湖门外吴侬家，郎若闲时来吃茶。
黄土筑墙茅盖屋，门前一树紫荆花

芦花被

采得芦花不浣尘，翠蓑聊复藉为茵。
西风刮梦秋无际，夜月生香雪满身。
毛骨已随天地老，声名不让古今贫。
青绫莫为鸳鸯妒，欸乃声中别有春！

桃花岩

美人一别三千年，思美人兮在我前。
桃花染雨入白兆，信知尘世逃神仙。
空山亭亭伴朝暮，老树悲啼发红雾。
为谁化作神仙区？十丈风烟挂淮浦。
暖翠流香春自活，手捻残霞皆细末。
几回云外落青啸，美人天上骑丹鹤。
神游八极栖此山，流水杳然心自闲。
解剑狂歌一壶外，知有洞府无人间。
酒酣仰天呼太白，眼空四海无纤物。
明月满山招断魂，春风何处求颜色？

别离情

吁别离之苦兮，苍梧之野春草青。
黄陵庙前春水生。
日暮湘裙动轻翠，玉树亭亭染红泪。
又闻垓下虞姬泣，斗帐初惊楚歌毕。
佳人阁泪弃英雄，剑血不销原草碧。
何物谓之别离情，肝肠剥剥如铜声。
不如斫其竹，翦其草，免使人生谓情老。

王冕

应教题梅

刺刺北风吹倒人，乾坤无处不沙尘。
胡儿冻死长城下，谁信江南别有春？

梅花

三月东风吹雪消，湖南山色翠如浇。
一声羌管无人见，无数梅花落野桥。

漫成

西邻昨夜哭暴卒，东家今日悲免官。
今日不知来日事，人生可放酒杯干？

相思

深情长是暗相随，月白风清苦苦思。
不似东姑痴醉酒，幕天席地了无知。

庐山瀑布谣

银河忽如瓠子决，泻诸五老之峰前。
我疑天仙织素练，素练脱轴垂青天。
便欲手把并州剪，剪取一幅玻璃烟。
相逢云石子，有似捉月仙。
酒喉无耐夜渴甚，骑鲸吸海枯桑田。
居然化作十万丈，玉虹倒挂清泠渊。

西湖竹枝歌

劝郎莫上南高峰，劝侬莫上北高峰。
南高峰云北高雨，云雨相催愁杀侬。

倪瓒

竹枝词二首

一

湖边女儿红粉妆，不学罗敷春采桑。
学成飞燕春风舞，嫁与燕山游冶郎。

二

阿翁闻说国兴亡，记得钱王与岳王。
日暮狂风吹柳折，满湖烟雨绿茫茫。

明 代

张以宁

严陵钓台

故人已乘赤龙去，君独羊裘钓月明。
鲁国高名悬宇宙，汉家小吏待公卿。
天回御榻星辰动，人去空台山水清。
我欲长竿数千尺，坐来东海看潮生。

宋濂

越歌

恋郎思郎非一朝，好似并州花剪刀。
一股在南一股北，几时裁得合欢袍？

晓行

荒鸡一再号，驱车事晨征。
寥寥秋风肃，况此华月明。
万顷琉璃中，着吾一身行。
肝胆尽冰雪，毛发亦含清。
超然鸿蒙初，顿觉百虑冥。
安得王子乔，为言此时情？

春蚕

可笑春蚕独苦辛，为谁成茧却焚身？
不如无用蜘蛛网，网尽蜚虫不畏人。

五月十九日大雨

风驱急雨洒高城，云压轻雷殷地声。
雨过不知龙去处，一池草色万蛙鸣。

客中夜坐

落叶萧萧江水长，故园归路更茫茫。
一声新雁三更雨，何处行人不断肠！

天平山中

细雨茸茸湿楝花，南风树树熟枇杷。
徐行不记山深浅，一路莺啼送到家。

岳阳楼

春色醉巴陵，阑干落洞庭。
水吞三楚白，山接九疑青。
空阔鱼龙舞，娉婷帝子灵。
何人夜吹笛？风急雨冥冥。

张羽

燕山春暮

金水桥边蜀鸟啼，玉泉山下柳花飞。
江南江北三千里，愁绝春归客未归。

徐贲

雨后慰池上芙蓉

池上新晴偶独过，芙蓉寂寞照寒波。
相看莫厌秋情薄，若在春风怨更多。

高启

水上盥手

盥手爱春水，水香手应绿。
沄沄细浪起，杳杳惊鱼伏。
怊怅坐沙边，流花去难掬。

梅花

琼姿只合在瑶台，谁向江南处处栽？
雪满山中高士卧，月明林下美人来。
寒依疏影萧萧竹，春掩残香漠漠苔。
自去何郎无好咏，东风愁寂几回开？

寻胡隐君

渡水复渡水，看花还看花。
春风江上路，不觉到君家。

田舍夜舂

新妇舂粮独睡迟，夜寒茅屋雨来时。
灯前每嘱儿休哭，明日行人要早炊。

解缙

赴广西别魏彭云路

多情为我谢彭郎，采石江深似渭阳。
相聚六年如梦过，不如昨夜一更长。

方孝孺

应召赴京道上有作

摇落秋冬际，苍茫鄞越间。
青山欹枕过，白鸟背人还。
问俗乡音异，消愁酒价悭。
虚名果何物？不使病夫闲。

于谦

石灰吟

千锤万击出深山，烈火焚烧若等闲。
粉骨碎身浑不怕，要留清白在人间。

除夜宿太原寒甚

寄语天涯客，轻寒底用愁？
春风来不远，只在屋东头。

沈周

折花仕女

去年人别花正开，今日花开人未回。
紫恨红愁千万种，春风吹入手中来。

李东阳

与钱太守诸公游岳麓寺四首席上作

其三

危峰高瞰楚江干，路在羊肠第几盘。
万树松杉双径合，四山风雨一僧寒。
平沙浅草连天远，落日孤城隔水看。
蓟北湘南俱入眼，鹧鸪声里独凭栏。

祝允明

口号二首

一

枝山老子鬓苍浪，万事遗来剩得狂。
从此日和先友对，十年汉晋十年唐。

二

不裳不袄不梳头，百遍回廊独步游。
步到中庭仰天卧，便如鱼子转瀛洲。

新春日

拂旦梅花发一枝，融融春气到茅茨。
有花有酒有吟咏，便是书生富贵时。

唐寅

阊门即事

世间乐土是吴中，中有阊门更擅雄。
翠袖三千楼上下，黄金百万水西东。
五更市买何曾绝？四远方言总不同。
若使画师描作画，画师应道画难工。

感怀

不炼金丹不坐禅，饥来吃饭倦来眠。
生涯画笔兼诗笔，踪迹花边与柳边。
镜里形骸春共老，灯前夫妇月同圆。
万场快乐千场醉，世上闲人地上仙。

桃花庵歌

桃花坞里桃花庵，桃花庵里桃花仙；
桃花仙人种桃树，又摘桃花换酒钱。
酒醒只在花前坐，酒醉还来花下眠；
半醉半醒日复日，花落花开年复年。
但愿老死花酒间，不愿鞠躬车马前；
车尘马足富者趣，酒盏花枝贫者缘。
若将富贵比贫者，一在平地一在天；
若将贫贱比车马，他得驱驰我得闲。
别人笑我忒风颠，我笑他人看不穿；
不见五陵豪杰墓？无花无酒锄作田。

一年歌

一年三百六十日，春夏秋冬各九十。

冬寒夏热最难当，寒则如刀热如炙。

春三秋九号温和，天气温和风雨多。

一年细算良辰少，况又难逢美景何？

美景良辰倘相遇，又有赏心并乐事；

不烧高烛对芳尊，也是虚生在人世。

古人有言亦达哉，劝人秉烛夜游来。

春宵一刻千金价，我道千金买不回。

文徵明

石湖

石湖烟水望中迷，湖上花深鸟乱啼。

芳草自生茶磨岭，画桥横注越来溪。

凉风袅袅青萍末，往事悠悠白日西。

依旧江波秋月坠，伤心莫唱《夜乌栖》。

李梦阳

秋望

黄河水绕汉边墙，河上秋风雁几行。
客子过壕追野马，将军弢箭射天狼。
黄尘古渡迷飞挽，白月横空冷战场。
闻道朔方多勇略，只今谁是郭汾阳？

王守仁

泛海

险夷原不滞胸中，何异浮云过太空。
夜静海涛三万里，月明飞锡下天风。

王廷相

古陵

古陵在蒿下，啼鸟在蒿上。
陵中人不闻，行客自惆怅。

边贡

重赠吴国宾

汉江明月照归人，万里秋风一叶身。
休把客衣轻浣濯，此中犹有帝京尘。

徐祯卿

偶见

深山曲路见桃花，马上匆匆日欲斜。
可奈玉鞭留不住，又衔春恨到天涯。

何景明

秋江词

烟渺渺，碧波远。白露晞，翠莎晚。
泛绿漪，蒹葭浅，浦风吹帽寒发短。
美人立，江中流。
暮雨帆樯江上舟，夕阳帘栊江上楼。
舟中采莲红藕香，楼前踏翠芳草愁。
芳草愁，西风起。芙蓉花，落秋水。
江白如练月如洗，醉下烟波千万里。

杨慎

柳

垂杨垂柳管芳年，飞絮飞花媚远天。
金距斗鸡寒食后，玉蛾翻雪暖风前。
别离江上还河上，抛掷桥边与路边。
游子魂销青塞月，美人肠断翠楼烟。

黄峨

又寄升庵

懒把音书寄日边，别离经岁又经年。
郎君自是无归计，何处青山不杜鹃！

谢榛

秋日怀弟

生涯怜汝自樵苏，时序惊心尚道途。
别后几年儿女大，望中千里弟兄孤。
秋天落木愁多少，夜雨残灯梦有无？
遥想故园挥涕泪，况闻寒雁下江湖。

吴承恩

对月感秋

人云天上月，中有嫦娥居。
孤栖与谁共？顾兔并蟾蜍。
冰轮不载土，桂树无根株。
纷纷黄金粟，岁岁何由舒？
一闭千万年，玉颜近何如？
相违不咫尺，照我阑干隅。
一杯劝尔酒，为我留须臾。

李攀龙

于郡城送明卿之江西

青枫飒飒雨凄凄，秋色遥看入楚迷。
谁向孤舟怜逐客？白云相送大江西。

杨继盛

登泰山

志欲小天下，特来登泰山。
仰观绝顶上，犹有白云还。

杨妃春睡图

守宫夜落胭脂臂，玉阶草色蜻蜓醉。
花气随风出御墙，无人知晓杨妃睡。
皂纱帐底绛罗委，一团红玉沉秋水。
画里犹能动世人，何怪当年走天子。
欲呼与语不得起，走向屏西打鹦鹉。
为向华清日影斜，梦里曾飞何处雨？

戚将军赠宝剑歌

毋嫌身价抵千金，一寸纯钩一寸心。
欲识命轻恩重处，灞陵风雨夜来深。

独坐

有客开青眼，无人问落花。
暖风熏细草，凉月照晴沙。
客久翻疑梦，朋来不忆家。
琴书犹未整，独坐送晚霞。

戚继光

晓征

霜溪曲曲转旌旗，几许沙鸥睡未知。
笳鼓声高寒吹起，深山惊杀老阇黎。

汤显祖

七夕醉答君东

玉茗堂开春翠屏，新词传唱《牡丹亭》。
伤心拍遍无人会，自掐檀痕教小伶。

高攀龙

枕石

心同流水净，身与白云轻。
寂寂深山暮，微闻钟磬声。

袁宏道

东阿道中晚望

东风吹绽红亭树，独上高原愁日暮。
可怜骊马蹄下尘，吹作游人眼中雾。
青山渐高日渐低，荒园冻雀一声啼。
三归台畔古碑没，项羽坟头石马嘶。

袁中道

夜泉

山白鸟忽鸣，石冷霜欲结。
流泉得月光，化为一溪雪。

冯小青

读《牡丹亭》绝句

冷雨幽窗不可听，挑灯闲看《牡丹亭》。
人间亦有痴于我，岂独伤心是小青。

陈子龙

孟秋十三夜

日暮维舟枫树林，玉峰峰外漏沉沉。
那堪独对当时月？泪落吴江秋水深。

夏完淳

别云间

三年羁旅客，今日又南冠。
无限河山泪，谁言天地宽？
已知泉路近，欲别故乡难。
毅魄归来日，灵旗空际看。

清代

钱谦益

留题秦淮丁家水阁

苑外杨花待暮潮，隔溪桃叶限红桥。
夕阳凝望春如水，丁字帘前是六朝。

咏同心兰

并头容易共心难，香草真当目以兰。
不似西陵凡草木，漫将啼眼引郎看。

柳如是

西湖

垂杨小院绣帘东，莺阁残枝蝶趁风。
大抵西泠寒食路，桃花得气美人中。

金圣叹

与儿子雍

与汝为亲妙在疏，如形随影只于书。
今朝疏到无疏地，无著天亲果宴如。

临别口号遍谢弥天大人谬知我者

东西南北海天疏，万里来寻圣叹书。
圣叹只留书种在，累君青眼看何如？

吴伟业

圆圆曲

鼎湖当日弃人间，破敌收京下玉关；
恸哭六军俱缟素，冲冠一怒为红颜。
红颜流落非吾恋，逆贼天亡自荒宴。
电扫黄巾定黑山，哭罢君亲再相见。
相见初经田窦家，侯门歌舞出如花。
许将戚里空侯伎，等取将军油壁车。
家本姑苏浣花里，圆圆小字娇罗绮。
梦向夫差苑里游，宫娥拥入君王起。
前身合是采莲人，门前一片横塘水。
横塘双桨去如飞，何处豪家强载归？
此际岂知非薄命，此时惟有泪沾衣。
熏天意气连宫掖，明眸皓齿无人惜。
夺归永巷闭良家，教就新声倾坐客。
坐客飞觞红日暮，一曲哀弦向谁诉？
白皙通侯最少年，拣取花枝屡回顾。

早携娇鸟出樊笼，待得银河几时渡？
恨杀军书抵死催，苦留后约将人误。
相约恩深相见难，一朝蚁贼满长安。
可怜思妇楼头柳，认作天边粉絮看。
遍索绿珠围内第，强呼绛树出雕栏。
若非壮士全师胜，争得蛾眉匹马还？
蛾眉马上传呼进，云鬟不整惊魂定；
蜡炬迎来在战场，啼妆满面残红印。
专征箫鼓向秦川，金牛道上车千乘；
斜谷云深起画楼，散关月落开妆镜。
传来消息满江乡，乌柏红经十度霜；
教曲妓师怜尚在，浣纱女伴忆同行。
旧巢共是衔泥燕，飞上枝头变凤皇。
长向尊前悲老大，有人夫婿擅侯王。
当时只受声名累，贵戚名豪尽延致。
一斛珠连万斛愁，关山漂泊腰支细。
错怨狂风飏落花，无边春色来天地。
尝闻倾国与倾城，翻使周郎受重名。
妻子岂应关大计？英雄无奈是多情。
全家白骨成灰土，一代红妆照汗青。
君不见馆娃初起鸳鸯宿，越女如花看不足。
香径尘生乌自啼，屟廊人去苔空绿。
换羽移宫万里愁，珠歌翠舞古梁州。
为君别唱吴宫曲，汉水东南日夜流！

阻雪

关山虽胜路难堪，才上征鞍又解骖。
十丈黄尘千尺雪，可知俱不似江南！

李渔

断肠诗哭亡姬乔氏

各事纷纷一笔销，安心蓬户伴渔樵。
赠予宛转情千缕，偿汝零星泪一瓢。
偕老愿终来世约，独栖甘度可怜宵。
休言再觅同心侣，岂复人间有二乔！

方以智

独往

同伴都分手，麻鞋独入林。
一年三变姓，十字九椎心。
听惯干戈信，愁因风雨深。
死生容易事，所痛为知音。

顾炎武

塞下曲

赵信城边雪化尘，纥干山下雀呼春。
即今三月莺花满，长作江南梦里人。

宋琬

舟中见猎犬有感

秋水芦花一片明，难同鹰隼共功名。
樯边饭饱垂头睡，也似英雄髀肉生。

龚鼎孳

上巳将过金陵

倚槛春愁玉树飘，空江铁锁野烟消。
兴怀何限兰亭感，流水青山送六朝。

顾媚

自题桃花杨柳图

郎道花红如妾面，妾言柳绿似郎衣。
何时得化鹡鸰鸟？拂叶穿花一处飞。

吴嘉纪

内人生日

潦倒丘园二十秋，亲炊葵藿慰余愁。
绝无暇日临青镜，频过凶年到白头。
海气荒凉门有燕，溪光摇荡屋如舟。
不能沽酒持相祝，依旧归来向尔谋。

施闰章

雪中阁望

江城草阁俯渔矶，雪满千山失翠微。
笑指白云来树杪，不知却是片帆飞。

王夫之

悼亡四首（选一）

十年前此晓霜天，惊破晨钟梦亦仙。
一断藕丝无续处，寒风落叶洒新阡。

叶燮

客发苕溪

客心如水水如愁，容易归舟趁疾流。
忽讶船窗送吴语，故山月已挂船头。

朱彝尊

来青轩

天书稠叠此山亭，往事犹传翠辇经。
莫倚危栏频北望，十三陵树几曾青？

屈大均

花前

花前小立影徘徊，风解吹裙百摺开。
已有泪光同白露，不须明月上衣来。

王士禛

再过露筋祠

翠羽明珰尚俨然，湖云祠树碧于烟。
行人系缆月初坠，门外野风开白莲。

秦淮杂诗

年来肠断秣陵舟，梦绕秦淮水上楼。
十日雨丝风片里，浓春烟景似残秋。

蒲松龄

次韵答王司寇阮亭先生见赠

志异书成共笑之，布袍萧索鬓如丝。
十年颇得黄州梦，冷雨寒灯夜话时。

洪升

客愁

夜夜贾舡里，思乡愁奈何。
醒听北人语，梦听南人歌。

孔尚任

北固山看大江

孤城铁瓮四山围，绝顶高秋坐落晖。
眼见长江趋大海，青天却似向西飞。

陈于王

《桃花扇传奇》题辞

玉树歌残迹已陈，南朝宫殿柳条新。
福王少小风流惯，不爱江山爱美人。

查慎行

青溪口号

来船桅杆高，去船橹声好。
上水厌滩多，下水惜滩少。

纳兰性德

秣陵怀古

山色江声共寂寥，十三陵树晚萧萧。
中原事业如江左，芳草何须怨六朝？

赵执信

秋暮吟望

小阁高栖老一枝，闲吟了不为秋悲。
寒山常带斜阳色，新月偏明落叶时。
烟水极天鸿有影，霜风卷地菊无姿。
二更短烛三升酒，北斗低横未拟窥。

沈德潜

过许州

到处陂塘决决流，垂杨百里罨平畴。
行人便觉须眉绿，一路蝉声过许州。

金农

柳

销魂桥外绿匆匆，树亦销魂客送空。
万缕千丝生便好，剪刀谁说胜春风？

厉鹗

湖楼题壁

水落山寒处，盈盈记踏春。
朱栏今已朽，何况倚栏人！

郑燮

竹石

咬定青山不放松，立根原在破岩中。
千磨万击还坚劲，任尔东西南北风！

潍县署中画竹呈年伯包大中丞括

衙斋卧听萧萧竹，疑是民间疾苦声。
些小吾曹州县吏，一枝一叶总关情。

倪瑞璇

闻蛙

草绿清池水面宽，终朝阁阁叫平安。
无人能脱征徭累，只有青蛙不属官。

曹雪芹

黛玉葬花辞

花谢花飞飞满天，红消香断有谁怜？
游丝软系飘春榭，落絮轻沾扑绣帘。
闺中女儿惜春暮，愁绪满怀无着处；
手把花锄出绣帘，忍踏落花来复去。
柳丝榆荚自芳菲，不管桃飘与李飞；
桃李明年能再发，明年闺中知有谁？
三月香巢初垒成，梁间燕子太无情！
明年花发虽可啄，却不道人去梁空巢也倾。
一年三百六十日，风刀霜剑严相逼；
明媚鲜妍能几时？一朝飘泊难寻觅。
花开易见落难寻，阶前愁杀葬花人；
独把花锄偷洒泪，洒上空枝见血痕。
杜鹃无语正黄昏，荷锄归去掩重门；

青灯照壁人初睡，冷雨敲窗被未温。

怪侬底事倍伤神，半为怜春半恼春；

怜春忽至恼忽去，至又无言去不闻。

昨宵庭外悲歌发，知是花魂与鸟魂？

花魂鸟魂总难留，鸟自无言花自羞；

愿侬此日生双翼，随花飞到天尽头。

天尽头！何处有香丘？

未若锦囊收艳骨，一抔净土掩风流；

质本洁来还洁去，不教污淖陷渠沟。

尔今死去侬收葬，未卜侬身何日丧？

侬今葬花人笑痴，他年葬侬知是谁？

试看春残花渐落，便是红颜老死时。

一朝春尽红颜老，花落人亡两不知！

袁枚

马嵬

莫唱当年《长恨歌》，人间亦自有银河。
石壕村里夫妻别，泪比长生殿上多。

遣兴

爱好由来下笔难，一诗千改始心安。
阿婆还似初笄女，头未梳成不许看。

鸡

养鸡纵鸡食，鸡肥乃烹之。
主人计固佳，不可使鸡知。

推窗

连宵风雨恶，蓬户不轻开。
山似相思久，推窗扑面来。

哭聪娘

记得歌成《陌上桑》，罗敷身许嫁王昌。

双栖吴苑三秋月，并走秦关万里霜。

羹是手调才有味，话无心曲不同商。

如何二十多年事，只抵春宵一梦长？

纪昀

富春至严陵山水甚佳

沿江无数好山迎，才出杭州眼便明。

两岸蒙蒙空翠合，琉璃镜里一帆行。

蒋士铨

题画

不写晴山写雨山，似呵明镜照烟鬟。

人间万象模糊好，风马云车便往还。

赵翼

论诗

李杜诗篇万口传，至今已觉不新鲜。

江山代有才人出，各领风骚数百年。

敦敏

赠曹雪芹

碧水青山曲径遐，薜萝门巷足烟霞。

寻诗人去留僧舍，卖画钱来付酒家。

燕市狂歌悲遇合，秦淮残梦忆繁华。

新愁旧恨知多少，一醉酕醄白眼斜。

姚鼐

江上竹枝词

东风送客上江船，西风催客下江船。

天公若肯如侬愿，便作西风吹一年。

胡亦常

游圭峰

群山乱几重，天半矗圭峰。
泉饮千岩石，云吞万壑松。
南溟奔绝岸，朝日起孤筇。
不觉一长啸，空潭吼卧龙。

黄景仁

别老母

搴帷拜母河梁去，白发愁看泪眼枯。
惨惨柴门风雪夜，此时有子不如无。

张维屏

新雷

造物无言却有情，每于寒尽觉春生。
千红万紫安排着，只待新雷第一声。

林则徐

出嘉峪关感赋

严关百尺界天西，万里征人驻马蹄。
飞阁遥连秦树直，缭垣斜压陇云低。
天山巉削摩肩立，瀚海苍茫入望迷。
谁道崤函千古险？回看只见一丸泥。

龚自珍

己亥杂诗之五

浩荡离愁白日斜，吟鞭东指即天涯。
落红不是无情物，化作春泥更护花。

己亥杂诗之一二五

九州生气恃风雷，万马齐喑究可哀。
我劝天公重抖擞，不拘一格降人才。

郑珍

自沾益出宣威入东川

出衙更似居衙苦，愁事堪当异事征。
逢树便停村便宿，与牛同寝豕同兴。
昨宵蚤会今宵蚤，前路蝇迎后路蝇。
任诩东坡渡东海，东川若到看公能。

黄遵宪

日本杂事诗

拔地摩天独立高，莲峰涌出海东涛。
二千五百年前雪，一白茫茫积未消。

谭嗣同

晨登衡岳祝融峰

身高殊不觉，四顾乃无峰。
但有浮云度，时时一荡胸。
地沉星尽没，天跃日初熔。
半勺洞庭水，秋寒欲起龙。

秋瑾

新风歌

秋风起兮百草黄，秋风之性劲且刚。
能使群花皆缩首，助他秋菊傲秋霜。
秋菊枝枝本黄种，重楼叠瓣风云涌。
秋月如镜照江明，一派清波敢摇动？
昨夜风风雨雨秋，秋霜秋露尽含愁。
青青有叶畏摇落，胡鸟悲鸣绕树头。
自是秋来最萧瑟，汉塞唐关秋思发。
塞外秋高马正肥，将军怒索黄金甲。
金甲披来战胡狗，胡奴百万回头走。
将军大笑呼汉儿，痛饮黄龙自由酒。

THEORY ON LITERARY TRANSLATION OF THE CHINESE SCHOOL

The theory on literary translation of the Chinese school owes its origin to traditional Chinese culture, including the Confucian and the Taoist school of thought respectively represented by *Thus Spoke the Master* and *Laws Divine and Human*.

It is said in the first chapter of *Laws Divine and Human* that truth can be known, but it may not be the truth you know, and that things may be named, but names are not the things. When applied to literary translation, this may mean that the theory on literary translation can be known, but it may not the unproven theory on the one hand, nor the scientific theory on the other, for neither literary translation nor its theory is science. As the names are not equal to the things, the translation cannot be equal to the original. As there is more difference than equivalence between the Chinese and the English language, the principle of equivalence can not be applied to the translation between them as between two occidental languages.

It is said in the last chapter of *Laws Divine and Human* that truthful words may not be beautiful and beautiful words may not be truthful. That is to say, there is contradiction between truth and beauty or between equivalence and excellence. A translation where equivalents are used may be called a faithful or truthful translation. When no equivalent can be found between two languages, the translator should make use of the best expressions or excellent expressions of the target language. That may be called theory of excellence.

In *Thus Spoke the Master*, Confucius said, "At seventy, I can do what I will without going beyond what is right." Professor Zhu Guangqian said that this has shown the mature state of an artist. I think it may also show the mature state of a literary translator. The literal translator has used the equivalents without going beyond the original in sound; the liberal translator has described the image without going beyond the original in sense; the literary translator has described the scene without going beyond reality. Not to go beyond the original is to be truthful or faithful, and the translator has reached the ordinary level of translation. To do what one will without going beyond the original is not only to be faithful but also to make his translation beautiful, in that case the translator has attained a higher level. To excel the original without going beyond the reality it describes is to attain the highest level.

What is literary translation? It is an art of solving the contradiction between faithfulness (or truth) and beauty. How to solve it? There are three methods, namely, equalization, generalization and particularization. When there is little or no contradition between truth and beauty, equalization or equivalents may be used. When there is contradction between them, generalization may be used to make the meaning clear, and particularization to make a deeper impression.

Confucius said in *Thus Spoke the Master* that it would be good to be understandable, better to be enjoyable and best to be delectable or delightful. When applied to literary translation, this principle means that an understandable translation is good, an enjoyable one is better and a delightful one is best. The ontology or theory of contradition between truth and beauty, the methodology or theory of equalization, generalization and particularization, and the teleology or theory of the understandable, the enjoyable and the delectable, all owe their origin to the Confucian and Taoist schools of thoughts.

But Confucius said less about what delight is and more about how to be delightful. In the beginning of *Thus Spoke the Master* he said it is delightful to acquire knowledge and put it into practice; In Chapter Six he told us how Yan Hui could find delight in reading though living in a humble lane with only a handful of rice to eat and a gourdful of water to drink; In Chapter Eleven, Zeng Xi told us his delight in an spring excursion. From these examples we can see Confucius' theory on delight or teleology, and his theory on practice or methodology. His theory is not scientific but artistic. Since literary translation is an art but not a branch of science, his theory can not only be applied to the practice but also to the theory of literary translation. As his theory has stood the test of time, it is as durable as scientific theories. A theorist on science who studies truth and the truthful should not go beyond what is truthful. A theorist on art or an artist who studies beauty and the beautiful may go beyond what is truthful and faithful.

The contradiction between truth and beauty in Chinese theory on literary translation has developed into a contradiction between equivalence and excellence. As Keats said, "Beauty is truth, truth beauty," we may even say beauty is a virtue, a kind of excellence. When we cannot find the equivalent, we may resort to generalization or particularization.

In short, literary translation is an art to create the beautiful. This is the epistemology of the Chinese school. The contradition between truth and beauty or between equivalence and excellence is its ontology; the theory on equalization, generalization and particularization is its triple methodology; and the theory of the understandable, the enjoyable and the delectable or delightful is its triple teleology.

Xu Yuanchong
Oct. 2011

代后记：中国学派的文学翻译理论

  中国学派的文学翻译理论源自中国的传统文化，主要包括儒家思想和道家思想，儒家思想的代表著作是《论语》，道家思想的代表著作是《老子道德经》。

  《老子道德经》第一章开始就说："道可道，非常道；名可名，非常名。"联系到翻译理论上来，就是说：翻译理论是可以知道的，是可以说得出来的，但不是只说得出来而经不起实践检验的空头理论，这就是中国学派翻译理论中的实践论。其次，文学翻译理论不能算科学理论（自然科学），与其说是社会科学理论，不如说是人文学科或艺术理论，这就是文学翻译的艺术论，也可以说是相对论。后六个字"名可名，非常名"应用到文学翻译理论上来，可以有两层意思：第一层是原文的文字是描写现实的，但并不等于现实，文字和现实之间还有距离，还有矛盾；第二层意思是译文和原文之间也有距离，也有矛盾，译文和原文所描写的现实之间，自然还有距离，还有矛盾。译文应该发挥译语优势，运用最好的译语表达方式，来和原文展开竞赛，使译文和现实的距离或矛盾小于原文和现实之间的矛盾，那就是超越原文了。这就是文学翻译理论中的优势论或优化论，超越论或竞赛论。文学翻译理论应该解决的不只是译文和原文在文字方面的矛盾，还要解决译文和原文所反映的现实之间的矛盾，这是文学翻译的本体论。

  一般翻译只要解决"真"或"信"或"似"的问题，文学翻译却要解决"真"或"信"和"美"之间的矛盾。原文反映的现实不只是言内之意，还有言外之意。中国的文学语言往往有言外之意，甚至还有言外之情。文学翻译理论也要解决译文和原文的言外之意、言外之情的矛盾。

《论语》说："知之者不如好之者，好之者不如乐之者。"知之，好之，乐之，这"三之论"是对艺术论的进一步说明。艺术论第一条原则要求译文忠实于原文所反映的现实，求的是真，可以使人知之；第二条原则要求用"三化"法来优化译文，求的是美，可以使人好之；第三条原则要求用"三美"来优化译文，尤其是译诗词，求的是意美、音美和形美，可以使人乐之。如果"不逾矩"的等化译文能使人知之（理解），那就达到了文学翻译的低标准，如从心所欲而不逾矩的浅化或深化的译文既能使人知之，又能使人好之（喜欢），那就达到了中标准；如果从心所欲的译文不但能使人知之，好之，还能使人乐之（愉快），那才达到了文学翻译的高标准。这也是中国译者对世界译论作出的贡献。

翻译艺术的规律是从心所欲而不逾矩。"矩"就是规矩，规律。但艺术规律却可以依人的主观意志而转移，是因为得到承认才算正确的。所以贝多芬说：为了更美，没有什么清规戒律不可打破。他所说的戒律不是科学规律，而是艺术规律。不能用科学规律来评论文学翻译。

孔子不大谈"什么是"（What?）而多谈"怎么做"（How?）。这是中国传统的方法论，比西方流传更久，影响更广，作用更大，并且经过了两三千年实践的考验。《论语》第一章中说："学而时习之，不亦说（悦，乐）乎！""学"是取得知识，"习"是实践。孔子只说学习实践可以得到乐趣，却不说什么是"乐"。这就是孔子的方法论，是中国文学翻译理论的依据。

总而言之，中国学派的文学翻译理论是研究老子提出的

"信"（似）"美"（优）矛盾的艺术（本体论），但"信"不限原文，还指原文所反映的现实，这是认识论，"信"由严复提出的"信达雅"发展到鲁迅提出"信顺"的直译，再发展到陈源的"三似"（形似，意似，神似），直到傅雷的"重神似不重形似"，这已经接近"美"了。"美"发展到鲁迅的"三美"（意美，音美，形美），再发展到林语堂提出的"忠实，通顺，美"，转化为朱生豪"传达原作意趣"的意译，直到茅盾提出的"美的享受"。孔子提出的"从心所欲"发展到郭沫若提出的创译论（好的翻译等于创作），以及钱钟书说的译文可以胜过原作的"化境"说，再发展到优化论，超越论，"三化"（等化，浅化，深化）方法论。孔子提出的"不逾矩"和老子说的"信言不美，美言不信"有同有异。老子"信美"并重，孔子"从心所欲"重于"不逾矩"，发展为朱光潜的"艺术论"，包括郭沫若说的"在信达之外，愈雅愈好。所谓'雅'不是高深或讲修饰，而是文学价值或艺术价值比较高。"直到茅盾说的："必须把文学翻译工作提高到艺术创造的水平。"孔子的"乐之"发展为胡适之的"愉快"说（翻译要使读者读得愉快），再发展到"三之"（知之，好之，乐之）目的论。这就是中国学派的文学翻译理论发展为"美化之艺术"（"三美"，"三化"，"三之"的艺术）的概况。

许渊冲
2011年10月

图书在版编目（CIP）数据

宋元明清诗选: 汉英对照 / 许渊冲译. — 北京: 五洲传播出版社,
2018.1

（许译中国经典诗文集）

ISBN 978-7-5085-3898-3

Ⅰ. ①宋… Ⅱ. ①许… Ⅲ. ①古典诗歌－诗集－中国－宋元时期
－汉、英 ②古典诗歌－诗集－中国－明清时代－汉、英
Ⅳ. ①H319.4：I

中国版本图书馆CIP数据核字(2017)第323715号

宋元明清诗选

译　　者：许渊冲
策划编辑：荆孝敏　郑　磊
责任编辑：王　峰
中文编辑：孟学文
英文编辑：马培武 张祯隆
装帧设计：北京正视文化艺术有限责任公司
出版发行：五洲传播出版社
地　　址：北京市海淀区北三环中路31号生产力大楼B座6层
邮　　编：100088
电　　话：010－82005927，010-82007837
网　　址：http://www.cicc.org.cn http://www.thatsbooks.com
印　　刷：北京京之杰印刷有限公司
版　　次：2012年1月第1版　2018年1月第2版第2次印刷
开　　本：140mm×210mm 1/32
印　　张：9.75
字　　数：250千字
书　　号：ISBN 978-7-5085-3898-3
定　　价：89.00元